M000081872

Ecstatic Trails

ALSO BY ROB CAMPBELL

Plato's Garage
The Serious Shopping Guide: Los Angeles

Ecstatic Trails

The 52 Best Day Hikes and Nature Walks
in and Around Los Angeles

Rob Campbell

 AN LA WEEKLY BOOK FOR ST. MARTIN'S GRIFFIN 🐾 *New York*

ECSTATIC TRAILS: THE 52 BEST DAY HIKES AND NATURE WALKS IN AND AROUND LOS ANGELES. Copyright © 2002 by Rob Campbell. All rights reserved. Printed in the United States of America. No part of this book may be used or reproduced in any manner whatsoever without written permission except in the case of brief quotations embodied in critical articles or reviews. For information, address St. Martin's Press, 175 Fifth Avenue, New York, N.Y. 10010.

LA Weekly Books is a trademark of LA Weekly Media, Inc.

www.stmartins.com

BOOK DESIGN BY AMANDA DEWEY

Library of Congress Cataloging-in-Publication Data

Campbell, Rob.
    Ecstatic trails : the 52 best day hikes and nature walks in and around Los Angeles / Rob Campbell—1st ed.
      p. cm.
    ISBN 0-312-28954-5
    1. Hiking—California—Los Angeles Region—Guidebooks. 2. Trails—California—Los Angeles Region—Guidebooks. 3. Los Angeles Region (Calif.)—Guidebooks. I. Title.
GV199.42.C22 L652 2002
796.51'09794'93—dc21   2002069351

First Edition: September 2002

10 9 8 7 6 5 4 3 2 1

Contents

Part III: Special Recommendations   263

༄

Hikes and sections of hikes that are recommended for . . .

Acknowledgments

Thank you to Philip, Lynnie, Michael, Hillary, Solveig, Lennart, Rafael, Jon, Daniel, Doug, Laura Dail, Elizabeth Beier, Michael Connor, and author/hiking expert Jerry Schad, whose comprehensive "Afoot and Afield" guidebooks have introduced me to many Southern California hiking zones over the years.

Introduction:
Hiking the Blues Away

Los Angeles is one of few major American cities blessed with extreme examples of nature's handiwork on all sides. Rising and undulating from below sea level to over 10,000 feet, the coast, canyons, and mountains surrounding and veining the urban sprawl represent as complicated and varied a chain of environments as do the communities they have shaped and continue to define. This book is a guide to some of the best explorations of this energetic, multifaceted landscape.

Every good hike brings out a bit of the explorer in a person; a really great hike can be a thorough exploration of both outer and inner worlds—nourishment and delight for the body, mind, and soul. When you are bored or tired, a hike perks you up. If you're overweight, hiking is the most pleasurably effective way to shed the pounds. Tired of the gym? Take a hike. And if you're stressed out, burned out, or just plain depressed, there is nothing like a hike to kick you out of your muddled, negative head. I speak from indelible experience on all accounts.

I know a New Age reverend who says there is a font of angels streaming from a secret opening in the base of the mountains to the north of Los Angeles. Though I'm wary of talk about angels and devils, there is a definite presence in the hills that cradle the sprawling city. The earth is volatile here, and it shows in the profuse flamboyance of its outward features, which still reverberate with the energy released in their creation. The entire spectrum of moods is expressed in the murmurs of the trees and the moaning of the rocks, now in gentle chromatic succession, now in symphony, now in a fit of cacophony; a mad mingling of all possibilities.

The hikes described in this book constitute a novel path to discovery or rediscovery of the environs of Los Angeles. All are easily accessible ways to alleviate the nagging chronic ailment that living in the city can often seem to be. Up in the mountains and down in the canyons, so close to the seething sprawl, yet so far, one's tensions melt, whether in view of a traffic jam lurching along a freeway far below, or in an enchanted hideaway that makes the mad modern world feel universes removed. Join me on a tour of my fifty-two favorite ways to hike away the L.A. blues.

Instructions:
A Guide to the Guide

The hikes in this book are arranged by approximate difficulty levels, from Level 1, containing easy hikes appropriate for everyone including children and the elderly, to Level 4, detailing sometimes offbeat adventures for ambitious hikers. You can work your way through the book as you would a video game or a rigorous spiritual quest; a workout plan or a destressing program; a treasure hunt or a collection of recipes for lovely days. You may also choose to do away with the structure altogether and briefly study maps and directions before striking out on your own. No matter how much or how little guidance you desire, you will find a fit in these pages.

Within levels, hikes follow a free-flowing path from least strenuous to most challenging, numbered throughout the book from 1 to 52, Hike 1 being the first hike of Level 1 and Hike 50 being the last of Level 4. Hikes 51 and 52 are a "bonus round" out-of-town weekend in a magical place not far from Los Angeles up the coast. In ranking I've taken into account factors such as distance, completion time, and elevation change, all listed along with driving coordinates as a preface to detailed hike directions, descriptions, and impressions following each individual hike map. The map pages are meant to be copied, or even torn out for take-along pocket references, as traveling light but prepared is key.

My assessment of each hike also includes more subjective factors such as ease of trail navigation and the overall involvement required of the hiker. These will vary according to experience, taste, and current state of mind. I've been known to hike ten miles blisteringly fast to work through a fit of anger without noticing a single plant. I've also often experienced a complete immersion in my surroundings, disappearing into each passing root and leaf, making it difficult to follow the trail because I don't want to think about its eventual end. All completion times and pace markers are quoted on a wide scale to take into account those who speedwalk without rest, those who enjoy a leisurely lookie-loo stroll with frequent, perhaps prolonged, stops and strays, and everyone in between. Elevation changes are given in total figures, including any uphill/downhill sections you might face between the actual low and high points of each hike.

Following the main part of the guide are indices that list hikes by desirable features, and preceding it are a few paragraphs of basic facts and suggestions—a quick review for the seasoned trooper, but invaluable to the inexperienced hiker. Now, as your mother might have said, get out of the house and go play outside!

Part 1

~≪

Environment and
Equipment

Terra, Flora, Fauna,
and Precautions

This book supplies idiosyncratic information about each hike's terrain, plant life, and wild animal population in the individual hike entries.

In the meantime, here are a few necessary basics:

Geologically, Los Angeles is a hotbed, as witnessed by the frequent activity of the San Andreas Faultline, among many less famous, but no less active, faults. The wide and densely populated L.A. basin is bordered to the west by a rugged coastline and to the north by a series of sparsely settled mountain ranges. These range from the rustic sandstone and slate-dominated Santa Monicas to the sometimes rounded, sometimes jagged, fast-growing and even faster-eroding, granite-rich San Gabriels in the east.

Though most of the Los Angeles region is designated a Mediterranean climate, joining only three to four percent of the world's landmass and typified by warm, sunny days nearly year-round with a very dry summer and a string of wet winter cold spells, several subclimates lurk among its dramatic topography.

Of most interest to hikers, the coastal zone, extending ten to fifteen miles inland along the Santa Monica Mountain range, tends to hold low-lying, view-obscuring fog until late morning and also stays cooler and moister during the summer. Conversely, the inland valleys, comprising the entire Los Angeles basin, tend to be more arid and extremely hot during dry summer and autumn months. Both of these subclimates receive ten to sixteen inches of rain on average each year, while the high country and mountainous zones experience approximately twice this amount, including snows that may begin as early as late November and stay on the ground, or even continue, until early May. These areas are not recommended for winter hiking unless you have had experience or training in snow and ice. Lower area subclimates are welcoming year-round—if overly hot for some in the summer—with some of the most comfortable, clearest, glistening days occurring in the sunny, dry stretches that always spring up in the sporadically wet winter months. I'll let you know what each hike is like in all seasons, and point out when one season is more enjoyable than the others.

Under this clement climate and its various subclimates, there are six major environment types I'll refer to:

Chaparral: California's dominant inland environment, covering hills, canyons, coastal ranges, and valleys throughout the region from 500 to about 5,000 feet, often to a height of over ten feet; characterized predominantly by scrub oak, manzanita, chamise, sage, laurel sumac, buckbrush, yucca whipplei or candlestick plant (referring to its towering, taperlike flower stalk), and toyon, the hollylike shrub that gave Hollywood its name; dry in the summer and rife with flowers and bees in the spring; home to various snakes—most famously the rattlesnake—rodents, coyotes, and small birds, plus the occasional antelope or mountain lion at higher elevations.

Coastal Scrub: Sometimes called "soft chaparral," this environment includes lusher, flowering plants and vines, such as the monkey flower and morning glory, with a predominance of sage and some of the best spring wildflowers in the area. It covers low-lying hilly areas adjacent to the coastline, mostly on south-facing slopes to an elevation of about 2,000 feet, and tends to be shorter and softer than "hard chaparral," its tall, bristly inland cousin. Wildlife populations in coastal scrub areas are similar to those of the chaparral.

Riparian Wilderness: A fancy way of designating a creekside area, found wherever creeks run, except in the many areas in which this rich habitat has been invaded or destroyed by the suburbs. Supremely pleasant, cool, and inviting, this type of environment is characterized by vines and leggy shrubs, including poison oak. This is also found in limited quantities in chaparral and coastal scrub areas, but grows profusely along almost all streams and lush canyons. If spacious enough, riparian wildernesses include fine, shady trees such as live oak, sycamore, white alder, bay laurel, spruce, elderberry, and California walnut, and many are quite overgrown and green all year long; home to a variety of frogs and toads, water insects, snakes, and birds.

Oak Woodlands/Oak Savannah: A meadowland studded with large communities of, usually, coast live oak, often at quite high elevations, larger ones often being accompanied by a small "flat," or reedy pond area. "Oak woodlands" describes a thinnish forest and "oak savannah" a meadowlands studded with trees. These environments are home to snakes, hawks, and rodents.

Grasslands: A completely self-explanatory environment type, similar, and sometimes interspersed with, oak savannah areas, but featuring taller grasses and, often, great joyous blankets of wild-flowers in the spring; wildlife as above, but with a larger snake population.

Coniferous Forest: Found in mountainous areas above 5,000 feet, and sometimes as low as 4,000 feet, the Los Angeles area's pine-dominated forests, inhabiting the often inhospitable San Gabriel mountain range, are sparser than those of the Sierra Nevadas and Rockies, which are commonly referred to in describing this type of environment. Here you will find a towering, open forest made up predominantly of Douglas fir, ponderosa pine, sugar pine, and cedar, peppered by live oaks, bays and pockets of chaparral scrub such as low-lying manzanita and mountain mahogany. At about 8,000 feet, the forest thins even further, with white fir, limber pine, and, most dramatically, lodgepole pine huddling together in sparse, wind-blown stands up to the treeline, which occurs at over 10,000 feet.

You may encounter any number of these environments all in one hike. You'll find the landscape and its features used as points of reference, interest, and inspiration in the fifty-two hikes that follow.

A few basic precautions should be used to ensure that you intrude upon these habitats without a trace. Leave the plants and animals alone and do not litter. Utilize common sense, and be aware of the following:

- Poison oak can be easily identified by its distinctive three-leaved stems. It grows as a leggy shrub or tree-clinging vine in canyons both dry and wet, as well as among coastal scrub. In summer and autumn, the leaves turn a dramatic, pale, translucent magenta, but its open stems are toxic even after these fall. Some people react quite weakly to them, or not at all, but for anyone prone to a strong reaction long pants are always recommended;

some might even go as far as a mandatory long-sleeved shirt as well, especially in riparian zones or in the winter when the bare stems are difficult to identify.

- Ticks are prevalent in chaparral, grassland, and some riparian areas. Contrary to popular belief, ticks do not jump. Instead they wait on shrubs and grasses for large mammals—either you, a horse, or a deer, for the most part—to brush against their perches so that they can climb aboard. Though Lyme disease, carried by deer ticks, is not as prevalent on the West Coast as on the East, it has become more so in the past ten years. Ticks can be tiny little things—anywhere from the size of a poppy seed to a lentil—and can be checked for by carefully examining any exposed areas of skin following a hike, especially ankles, calves, and lower arms, using your fingers to sense any critters that might be light-colored or hiding among hair. If you find one, grip it lightly but firmly at its insertion point in your skin with a pair of tweezers. Pull it out carefully, being sure to free its entire snout.

- Rattlesnakes can be chanced upon almost anywhere, especially in the chaparral and grasslands during the dry summer and early autumn months. Some species of rattlers have evolved not to rattle when approached; even those who do rattle don't do so until you're just about to cross their paths, so it's best to keep a close eye out upon the land you're walking. Always give snakes the right of way.

- Mountain lions are rarely spotted. I have seen one—and that from a safe distance of a few hundred yards—in my twenty years of fairly regular exploration of the wilds of the Los Angeles area. They tend to be secretive, coming out only at dawn or dusk to hunt and patrol, but can be met during the day as well, usually in rocky high country or low to mid-mountain settings. If you are lucky enough to run into one of these awesome creatures, give it all the respect and space you would a ferocious escaped tiger from the circus. The mountain lion is truly king of its habitat, and considers any living creature a possible meal, including you, if it thinks it can take you on successfully. If you run, it will chase you. The best thing to do is to back away slowly and quietly, avoiding eye contact. Above all mind your own business—even casual, passing eye contact can provoke this big, wild cat.

- Deer are so skittish that their extreme reactions to any approach whatsoever can startle one to distraction—a dangerous proposition if your trail abuts a chasm or cliff. Be quiet and walk softly around these gentle, nervous creatures.

- Coyotes, common in all areas of Southern California, are also skittish, despite popular lore. Their yaps and howls are sometimes eerie, sometimes comforting, and can be heard usually during the dawn or dusk hours, when they will scamper away with their tails between their legs if you cross their paths. Coyotes have successfully inhabited even city-bordered wild regions, and will sometimes sneak into the backyards of canyon or countryside suburbs to snatch small pets and such, which has earned them a "pest" appellation according to many homeowners.

- Other hikers, while surprisingly rare in the wilds of Los Angeles, are sometimes chanced upon. In these instances, the common laws of hiking courtesy should be invoked: Yield to downhill hikers on narrow paths, and always yield to horses and their riders on equestrian or multipurpose trails. Mountain bikers should yield to both hikers and horses where biking is also permitted. Remain on trails when provided, especially making sure not to improvise shortcuts in delicately terrained or foliaged areas, and report any problems with trails to the national, state, county, or city park or conservancy responsible for their upkeep, as most are maintained by volunteers on call rather than on a regular, professional schedule. Do not be surprised should you run into a few places even on ostensibly wide, easygoing paths where some light bushwhacking is required, as chaparral grows in thick, bristly, and hardy when cut back and then left alone for a while.

What to Wear, Bring,
Drink, and Eat

There are a few very important but easily acquired basic pieces of equipment and supplies to consider when planning to hike.

First, you'll want to buy a really good pair of hiking shoes. Even one medium-length hike in a cheap pair of boots and you're hobbling around for a week. Get something that cushions and supports the foot, with a good, thick, gripping sole; high-rise if you prefer the ankle support. My favorite, after trying several types, is the Timberland "Active Comfort Technology" line of all-terrain shoes, sold for around a hundred dollars. Nike, CAT, and Clarks also do some good, solid hiking-appropriate styles. Spend the money and save your soles—hiking is extremely hard on the feet. Thick, cushioned socks help, too.

As for clothing, medium to lightweight cotton is most comfortable, with warmer layers carried along in your pack or tied about the waist. Denim is not fabulous for hiking unless you are doing heavy bushwhacking, nor is wool unless you are in the high country during late autumn or early spring, when sudden cold snaps can rise out of nowhere. You want your body to breathe, but you want to be able to keep out the cold if you have to, as well as shield yourself from the sun (did I mention sunscreen?). I advise long, loose-fitting pants, though I always wear cargo shorts myself, which is why my legs are so scratched up. Long pants also protect you from poison oak and ticks.

Next, think about the type of bag, knapsack, satchel, or even cargo pockets in which you're going to want to carry the various necessary things a hike dictates. This one's up to you, but I advise against anything that straps over only one shoulder or impedes the movement of any of your limbs.

To fill your carrying vessel, at the very least, you're going to want to bring water. If you are only bringing water and nothing else, which you very well may decide to do on shorter hikes, a *bota* bag, or Spanish wineskin, available in one or two liter sizes at any army/navy surplus store and some camping supply outlets, is perfect strapped across the chest, much lighter than a traditional canteen (which are usually made of metal), and easier to carry than a plastic bottle. Another good choice is a fancy, neoprene plastic bottle carrier.

On longer hikes, take along two to four liters of water, most easily, lightly, and sturdily in one-liter plastic bottles stowed in your rucksack. You will burn 400 to 800 calories an hour hiking, depending on your pace and the number and steepness of ascents, so bring plenty of protein bars, trail mix, jerky, or whatever lightweight, nonperishable snack item you like. You need fuel for your journey, even if you are trying to shed unwanted pounds.

Other useful items include a map, sunglasses, a small flashlight—especially on hikes that may take you past twilight—lip

balm, sunscreen, tissues or a handkerchief, some antibiotic oint-
ment and a few Band-Aids or a miniature first-aid kit for those
occasional scrapes and cuts, a compass, a watch, a pair of binoculars,
and a camera, if you wish, all of which can be easily stowed in a
smallish backpack. For avid picnickers, backpack-style picnic gear
for two to four can be found at most sports or camping emporia.
You'll figure out what you really want and need and how you like
to carry it as you establish your own hiking style and guidelines.

Minimal parking fees are sometimes required, which will be
noted adjacent to the driving directions for each hike; a National
Forest Adventure Pass is always required in the Angeles, San
Bernardino, and Cleveland Forests. Contact the Angeles Forest
at (626) 574-5200 for details, or consult a list of pass vendors on
the Internet at *http://r05s001.pswfs.gov/angeles/visitor/adventurepass/
adventurepass.html.*

Set out prepared, be safe, and have fun.

Part 2

The Hikes

Los Angeles Area Map

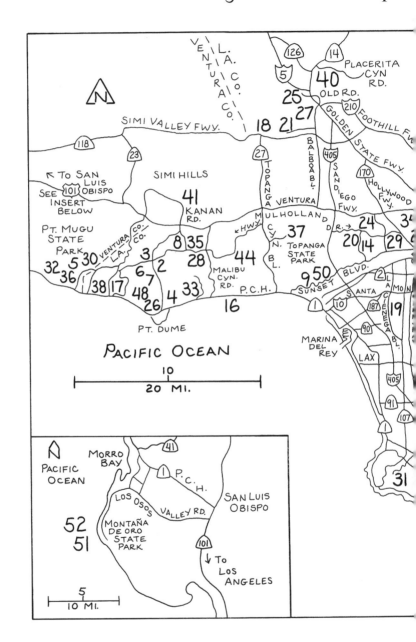

Hikes Located by Number

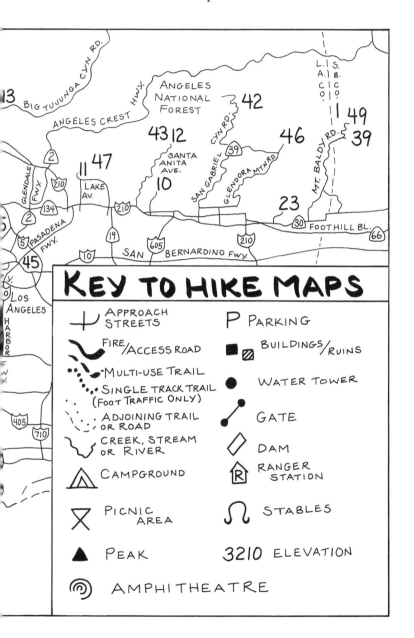

KEY TO HIKE MAPS

┼	APPROACH STREETS
(curved line)	FIRE/ACCESS ROAD
▪▪▪	MULTI-USE TRAIL
⋯	SINGLE TRACK TRAIL (FOOT TRAFFIC ONLY)
⋰	ADJOINING TRAIL OR ROAD
(wavy line)	CREEK, STREAM OR RIVER
△	CAMPGROUND
✕	PICNIC AREA
▲	PEAK
◎	AMPHITHEATRE
P	PARKING
■ ▨	BUILDINGS/RUINS
●	WATER TOWER
⊶	GATE
◇	DAM
Ⓡ	RANGER STATION
♫	STABLES
3210	ELEVATION

Map labels: BIG TUJUNGA CYN. RD., ANGELES CREST HWY., ANGELES NATIONAL FOREST, SANTA ANITA AVE., LAKE AV., GLENDALE FWY., PASADENA FWY., SAN GABRIEL CYN RD., GLENDORA MTN RD., MT. BALDY RD., L.A. CO. / S.B. CO., FOOTHILL BL., SAN BERNARDINO FWY., LOS ANGELES, HARBOR FWY.

Highway markers: 13, 2, 210, 134, 2, 5, 45, 10, 19, 605, 210, 30, 66, 405, 710

Hike numbers: 13, 42, 43, 12, 46, 1, 49, 39, 11, 47, 10, 39, 23, 45

LEVEL 1:

Waterfalls, Ranches, and Walks in the Park

Short and sweet; all appropriate for families with children and elders; great for picnicking, quick pick-me-ups, and romantic strolling.

⚘ SAN ANTONIO FALLS
Level 1, Hike 1

A brisk hill leads to these 100-foot falls below Mt. Baldy in the eastern high country, with a large, rocky bed at their base to explore

DISTANCE: 1.4 total miles: .6 miles one way and back, .2 mile sidetrip to base; Elevation change: 250 feet to falls only; 350 feet including sidetrip
DURATION: 30 minutes–1.5 hours
NOTES: Dawn-dusk; road sometimes closed during snow; dogs on leash permitted

DRIVING DIRECTIONS: Take the 210 Freeway east to its terminus as it blends into the 30 east, to its terminus at Foothill Boulevard; continue east to a left (north) on Mills Avenue; shallow right to Mt. Baldy Road at first stop sign. A steep, winding few miles, especially just after passing Icehouse Canyon turnoff, to 6,160 feet; park off-street where San Antonio Falls Road begins at left (west) past Manker Flats Campground; National Forest Adventure Pass required.

One of the tallest and strongest waterfalls in the region, San Antonio Falls plummets down a vertical, three-tiered granite runway after rains, and manages to keep up a low-key show throughout the dusty summer and dry early autumn.

You begin on San Antonio Falls Road where it leads straight up toward a locked pipe gate, past a row of outhouses to your left. Swing around the gate and head uphill on the graded gravel and

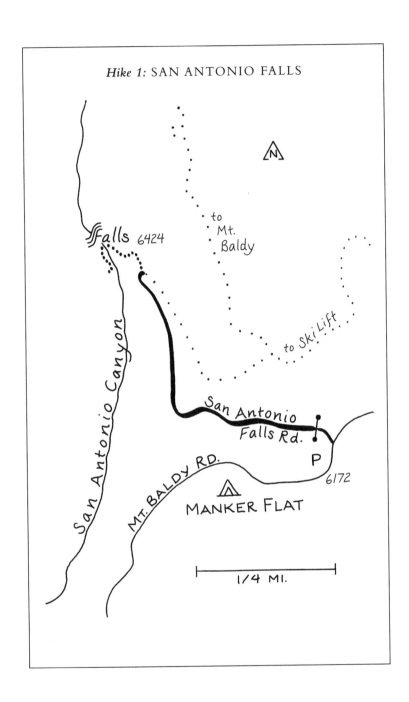

Hike 1: SAN ANTONIO FALLS

dirt road, open only to ski maintenance vehicles. You pass tall pines, some framing and shading rustic private cabins down to your left. The grade of the wide path is just challenging enough to work up a light sweat, and representative of the moderate grades you will encounter in these first two levels of hikes.

At 6,400 feet, you reach a spacious viewing area for the falls, now straight ahead across a wide wash of granite slabs and boulders studded with dense clumps of manzanita and other high-chaparral scrub. The road here hairpins up to your right, continuing to the ski-lift staging area and the turnoff for the trail to Mt. Baldy (Level 4, Hike 49), whose bare spine hovers directly above you at over 10,000 feet. You may prefer to sit or lean on one of the rocks here, content to be soothed by the constant flow of the spectacle.

For more intimate communion with the falls, follow the trail that leads off ahead of you to your right, precariously down along the canyon wall to the bed. This narrow foot-trail can be slippery at any time, and the bed potentially dangerous after heavy rainfall, so you'll want to keep a tight reign and a close eye on any children in your party, who will undoubtedly want to get as close as they can to the place where the falls hit not a pool, but a scattered stream-head pile of granite slabs that creak and clatter in rhythm to the constant rush of the water. The creek bed that leads away from the falls, while not conducive to picnicking, is an easily navigable, just-wild-enough environment, perfect for young explorers.

Simply retrace your steps to reach your starting point once you recover from the trance that tumbling water tends to induce.

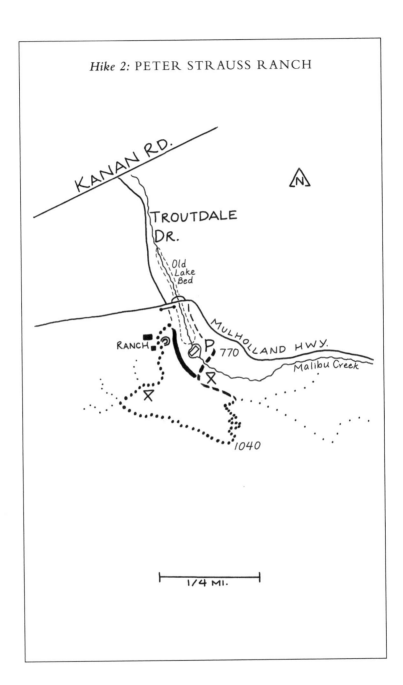

Hike 2: PETER STRAUSS RANCH

KANAN RD.

TROUTDALE DR.

Old Lake Bed

MULHOLLAND HWY.

RANCH

P 770

Malibu Creek

1040

N

1/4 MI.

❧PETER STRAUSS RANCH
Level 1, Hike 2

A short, sweet loop, plus a playground and picnicking on a fragrant hillside woodland at the western end of the Malibu Creek area

> DISTANCE: 1-mile loop, with sidetrips of varying length available near the starting point; Elevation change: 270 feet
> DURATION: 15–45 minutes
> NOTES: 8 A.M.–5 P.M.; dogs on leash permitted

DRIVING DIRECTIONS: Take Kanan Road exit south from the 101 Freeway to a left (west) at Troutdale Road and another left shortly thereafter on Mulholland Highway. Cross the bridge and turn right (south) into the large, signed dirt parking area, heading to your left, down toward the creekbed to beach your vehicle; no fee.

Actor/producer Peter Strauss owned this sixty-five-acre property before handing it over to the Santa Monica Mountains Conservancy in 1983. Up until the fifties it was the site of man-made Lake Enchanto, an exclusive, early Malibu-area resort. The lake is no longer apparent, but its long-unused dam is your landmark for this shady, uplifting little hike through a cool, enchanting coastal forest riddled with romantic hideaways and secret places for young adventurers to explore.

From the parking area, you can see the ruins of the dam in the center of the wide creekbed, which is usually dry and easily crossable in summer, and more involvingly forded during the wet season on a series of rocks, logs, and islets. Once over the creek, you come to a small playground nestled in a grove of eucalyptus; beyond it is the sign for the trail. Swing left and begin the trail here. The eucalyptus smells so good . . .

After a brief, strenuous climb you come to your first intersection. Make a sharp right uphill. The trail connects to a plethora of paths that vein the creekbed and lead nowhere in particular but can be fun to explore if you have the time and inclination. The Strauss trail winds up over rocks and graded railroad tie stairs to a lush tree-lined path, cool and inviting year-round.

You come to a fork after winding your way across the midsection of the hillside. Take the trail to your far right, which leads downhill onto the ranch grounds. You head down more wooden stairways, across a little wooden bridge and a huge fallen oak, and down to your left at the next fork. The trail to your right leads to a small picnic area, which is secluded in a thicket directly in the middle of the property. The trail is well laid out and graded, and not heavily used except by local early morning dog exercisers. It can be walked as a solitary stroll, with your sweetie during late-autumn dusk just before the gates close for a romantic effect, with children, or even as an exercise circuit, as many times around as you wish, for power walking or jogging.

Go down to the right at the next fork toward eucalypti and oak trees. There's a wonderful semideserted amphitheater here, occasionally used for special events and performances, perfect for meditation and yoga. Wander around the grounds, including the ranch house itself, also open only during special events, an enclosed aviary, now defunct, and a rustic bathhouse adjacent to the long-empty swimming pool. In front of the house is a wide, well-manicured lawn, utterly surreal in this wild, natural setting. To get back to your car, follow the drive beyond the cactus island garden to the sidewalk, right to the playground, and left over the creekbed.

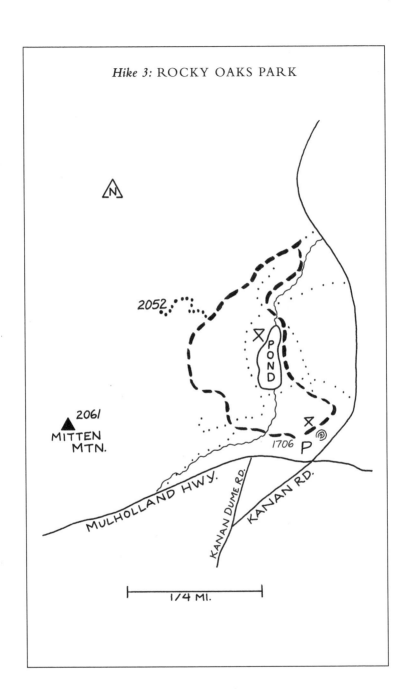

Hike 3: ROCKY OAKS PARK

N

2052

2061
MITTEN
MTN.

POND

1706
P

MULHOLLAND HWY.

KANAN DUME RD.

KANAN RD.

1/4 MI.

ROCKY OAKS PARK
Level 1, Hike 3

A rugged chaparral-laden loop with various mini-adventure sidetrails,
picnicking, and even sunbathing by this once-private property's large pond

DISTANCE: 1.2-mile loop, with sidetrips of varying
length along the route; Elevation change: 350 feet
DURATION: 20 minutes–1 hour
NOTES: 8 A.M.–dusk; dogs on leash permitted

DRIVING DIRECTIONS: Take Kanan Road exit south from the
101 Freeway to a right (west) on Mulholland Highway. The park is
on this corner; enter immediately to your right at the sign, and
park in the small dirt lot near the restrooms; no fee.

Beginning your hike at the Rocky Oaks Loop Trail marker on the
north side of the tiny parking area, you soon discover that this
jewellike 200-plus-acre park, once a cattle ranch and completely
burned over in the late 1970s, is laced with trails, all of them worth
a stray from the short but eclectic loop described here.

Go left at the first major fork, and you find the first of these
trails: It cuts straight through a tall grassland to a quiet, secluded and
overgrown riparian zone rife with hermit-friendly hideouts down
along the creek. Mitten Mountain, named for its obvious shape, is
straight ahead of you. This trail ends among some unidentifiable
machinery ruins at the fenced western perimeter of the park.

To continue on the loop, take the center prong of the fork—
the trail to your right leads down through grassland and meadow to

the pond, which we'll explore later. This center trail cuts quickly uphill through tall and often overgrown scrub oak, chamise, and sage. Near its apex you find the small Overlook Trail, with its somewhat hidden sign, leading up to the left. This short spur takes you quickly to the highest point in the park and a pleasant view from among a thicket of fragrant chaparral plants.

The main trail continues downhill to the northern perimeter of the park, where a chain-link fence runs along Kanan Road. Make a sharp right downhill toward the pond and its surrounding rocky meadowland, where ducks, geese, and mudhens quack and honk it out for water rights. The trail to your right takes you to a shady picnic plateau on the west side of the pond, but the east side of the pond, reached by the trail to your left, is far more interesting, with a procession of odd biomorphic rock formations and a small, perfectly flat, private, and comfortable beach when the water in the pond recedes during warm months—unbeatable for solitary sunbathing.

Walk right along the water's edge, take a left at the fork immediately after the pond, and a left again immediately after that, heading straight across the Loop Trail onto the Glade Trail connector. Soon you enter a spacious, extremely shady oak woodland with various picnic table areas and sidetrails to explore. The quickest way back to your car is to your right through the glade, along a sandy trail to an open amphitheater and drinking fountain area that borders the east side of the parking lot, where you exit the dense canopy of hardy oaks into the sunlight once more.

☙ ESCONDIDO FALLS
Level 1, Hike 4

A healthy walk through Malibu ranchland down through a lush canyon to a richly colored, storybook setting at the foot of this elegant, 200-plus-foot waterfall

DISTANCE: 3.6 miles: 1.8 miles one way and back;
Elevation change: 360 feet
DURATION: 1–2 hours
NOTES: No time restrictions; dogs on leash permitted

DRIVING DIRECTIONS: Take Pacific Coast Highway (PCH) north past Malibu Canyon Road to a right on Winding Way, just before Zuma Beach, and an immediate left into the signed and paved parking lot for the Escondido Canyon Natural Area; no fee.

Though almost a mile of this trail leads along the side of Winding Way, a private drive through a series of palatial-to-ramshackle Malibu ranch estates that allows for no public parking, Escondido Canyon and its fantastic falls are well worth the trip. The trail begins on the left side of Winding Way and crosses to the right at number 27725. Stay on the trail, as you're surrounded by private property.

Just past 27445/27465 Winding Way, a sign on your left announces your entry into the Santa Monica Mountains Conservancy Parkland. Follow the road uphill a bit more past the open field to your left; the deep, thickly-treed canyon will appear

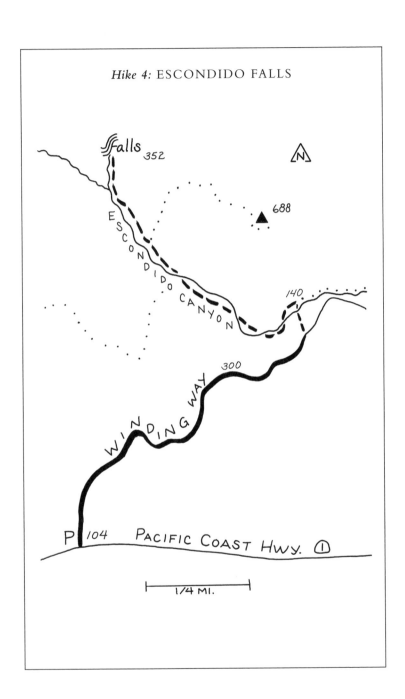

Hike 4: ESCONDIDO FALLS

beyond it. At the curve in the road, just past 27326, there is a steep loose-dirt trail that cuts down into the canyon to your left. You head downhill to a series of gulleys, and cross the often wet and/or muddy creek for the first of many times to hit a T-intersection where you turn left. The trail to your right explores the canyon for about half a mile to a dead end.

Now you're in an overgrown and lush riparian wilderness on your way to Escondido Falls. You pass under coast live oaks with their usual attendant sycamores and scrub oak, interspersed with random sprays and manicured-looking archways of chamise and manzanita. Crossing the creek a couple more times, you find plenty of bankside lounging or picnicking options underneath or in the crooks of the magnificent large oaks. You make your way around or under a fallen oak that was struck by lightning, keeping left at the fork just beyond it, then curve up past a sign that warns against motorbiking, and make another left at the T-intersection at the top of the hill. The stream now rushes noisily below you to your left; coyotes may be yapping in the grassy hills to your right.

The stream's invitation becomes more appealing as you near the falls, its plant life even more lush and viny. Sheer red-hued sandstone walls rise hundreds of feet straight above. The falls themselves appear as a perfect set for a *plein air* production of *A Midsummer Night's Dream*. The 200-foot cascade of water, a peaceful but complicated dribble in all seasons except just after heavy rains, wends and webs its way down the multicolored opalescence of a broken sandstone cliff into a generous ferny pool. The waterfall is flanked on one side by a large, comfortable, nearly perfectly rounded hillside shaded by a magisterial oak adorned with a swing strong enough for adults to play on. Its extreme picturesqueness makes Escondido Falls quite crowded on weekends and holidays, so if you want this magical place to yourself, come on a weekday or in the winter, when the site becomes an eerie echo chamber of trickling water.

To retrace the trail to the road, go right at the first fork before the large dry plateau, and walk along the trail until you see a blue-and-white house ahead and above you; turn right back up the hill to another right onto Winding Way.

✂ THE GROTTO AT CIRCLE X RANCH
Level 1, Hike 5

A hilly romp along the border between a lush canyon and an imposing hillside of high chaparral, then creekside to a cool, chapel-like confluence of trees and boulders

DISTANCE: 3 miles total: 1.4 miles one way and back, plus .1 mile of elective rock climbing; Elevation change: 700 feet

DURATION: 1–2 hours

NOTES: Dawn–dusk; dogs on leash permitted

DRIVING DIRECTIONS: Take the PCH north all the way to Yerba Buena Road, just past the Ventura County line. Turn right for a winding few miles to the easily-spottable sign for the 1,655-acre Circle X Ranch on the right. Park beside the ranger's station; no fee. To your right are restrooms, and a short trail to a vista point. Maps are available.

Thousands of Boy Scouts tromped the trails that riddle Circle X Ranch before the Boy Scouts of America handed it over to the National Parks Service in the 1980s. The trail to the Grotto begins to your left, down the service road to the campground parking area; follow the arrow to your left when you reach the solar energy outpost building. You pass by two wooden outhouses toward a sign reading CAMPGROUND PARKING ONLY, and a smaller sign to its right

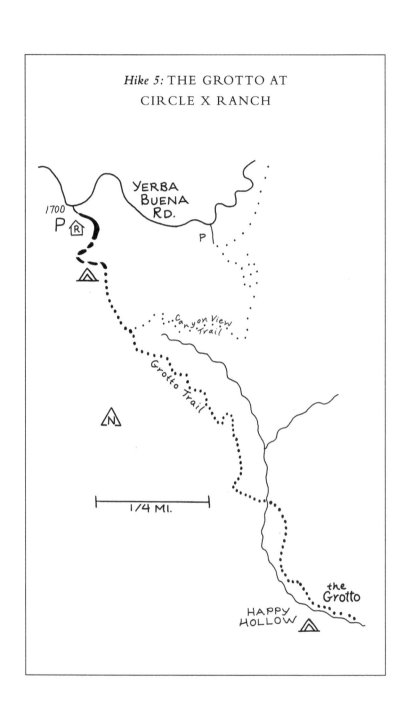

Hike 5: THE GROTTO AT
CIRCLE X RANCH

YERBA
BUENA
RD.

1700
P
R

P

Canyon View
Trail

Grotto Trail

N

1/4 MI.

the
Grotto

HAPPY
HOLLOW

reading GROTTO TRAILHEAD—CANYON VIEW TRAIL .4 MILES, THE GROTTO, 1.3 MILES. You immediately descend into a lovely canyon full of willows and sycamore and oak, crossing a creek, and traipsing along the border of the riparian and chaparral wildernesses, through a copse of pine.

Just beyond the copse is the Canyon View Trail turnoff; pass this and turn right to cross the creek again, where a lively waterfall flows during the wet season. Dip down and back up the hillside along the other side of the creek, with amazing views of the mountains straight ahead of you. You traverse a hilltop grassland on a faded asphalt spine, then out to a small vista point where you can look down on the canyon and its sheer, imposing rock formations. The trail continues on a shallow right in the same direction among chamise and manzanita, then turns sharply down into the canyon. Small dead-end sidetrails lead off everywhere. Watch for falling and fallen rock on the trail as you hug the canyon wall.

Keep descending into the shade of a giant oak as the trail curves right to take in an arm of the canyon, at the end of which you switchback left and descend all the way down. There may be a sign here reading TRAIL TO GROTTO, which was fallen last time I was there; keep left down into the canyon at the fork. You dip down and cross the creek again, past a sign warning of rattlesnakes, and another as the trail bends left at a sign reading THE GROTTO, .6 MILES, GROTTO TRAIL. You leave the creekbed again and descend once more under a canopy of oaks, where a wide leafy plateau signifies the Happy Hollow Campground (permit only, pack-in, pack-out). There's a trail off to your right here where you can make your way up the creekbed. The Grotto is just to your left down the trail, where the creek forms pools and cascades all year long. There are huge boulders to climb in the Grotto, out as far as a big flat staging area for a large wet-season waterfall. The creek can be navigated from this point as far as you like at your own risk, with some gnarly rock-climbing that is well worth the scenic pay-off. The rocks are extremely stable, but slippery when wet.

To get back to your car, simply make your way back across the rocks and up the creek on the same trail. The Grotto is a wonderful place to hide away for the whole day, or to bring the family for a picnic, and a compelling haven for rambunctious children.

✿ ARROYO SEQUIT PARK
Level 1, Hike 6

A mini-rollercoaster of a loop around this charming 155-acre property through high, arching chaparral and a sidetrip through riparian sycamore woodland

> **DISTANCE:** 2 miles total: 1.4-mile loop plus .6 miles of elective creekside sidetrails; Elevation change: 400 feet total, up and down all the way
> **DURATION:** 45 minutes–1.5 hours
> **NOTES:** 8 A.M.–dusk; dogs on leash permitted

DRIVING DIRECTIONS: The address of this small park is 34138 Mulholland Highway, which you can reach by taking the 101 to a southward exit at Topanga Boulevard or Kanan Road, and turning right on Mulholland, or by taking PCH north all the way to where Mulholland hits the beach, and turning right. Look for mile marker 5.6 and the addressed mailbox on your right if you're coming from the beach, or your left if you're coming from the freeway. Park in the small dirt area beside the National Parks Service sign, which features a map of park trails; no fee.

Walk up the road from the parking area through dry coastal scrub, amazingly green and profuse after rains. A fenced private residence appears ahead of you, and there are beautiful views of the mountains to your right. You curve left where a sign reading NATURE TRAIL—.2 MILES stands on the right. Follow the road past the white park building and the picnic ground, now curving to your right, past the

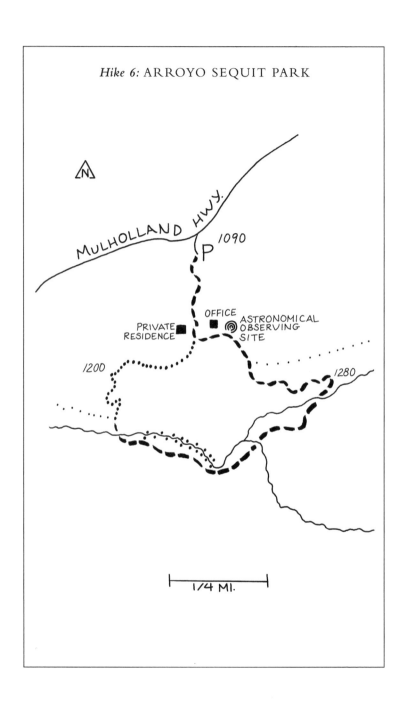

Hike 6: ARROYO SEQUIT PARK

N

MULHOLLAND HWY.

P 1090

OFFICE

PRIVATE
RESIDENCE

ASTRONOMICAL
OBSERVING
SITE

1200

1280

1/4 MI.

Santa Monica College Astronomical Observing Site with its ring of stone benches. From its attendant placard: THIS OPEN AREA, FAR FROM THE CITY LIGHTS OF LOS ANGELES, IS IDEAL FOR STARGAZING. SANTA MONICA COLLEGE HOLDS REGULAR TELESCOPE OBSERVING SESSIONS HERE. CONTACT ASTRONOMY DEPT. FOR DATES AND TIMES.

You continue on the road under a canopy of coast live oaks, and soon after will see a sign for the nature trail leading off to your right from the main road. Foliage markers line the path, alerting you to features such as grassland, purple sage, California sagebrush, and black sage. Unshaded picnic tables dot the trail.

The trail dips and curves over small hills to a lusher coastal chaparral, with little sidetrails into the brush. This is a great place for kids, but the trail is completely unshaded, so go on a cool day. Walking through the arches of chamise and manzanita feels rather like being part of a fairyland processional. There is a sinuous wind to the trail as you rise above a canyon filled with large manzanita and elegant sycamores and spruce. A smattering of untended footpaths lead down to the riparian wilderness below for shaded exploration and tranquility.

Shortly after rising beyond the sycamore canyon, you come to a sign facing the opposite direction reading NATURE TRAIL—END. Continue straight through, bearing to your right. The trail to your left leads out to a feeder road off Mulholland Highway.

Here the trail ascends quite steeply for a short while on switchbacks. A site of fire and regrowth is analyzed through small placards at the top of the hill, after which the trail dips right back down to the private residence that you passed at the beginning of your walk. You can also do this hike in the opposite direction if you wish, cutting in through the clearing between toyon trees at the sign on the first curve of the road. Turn left on the road to reach the park entrance.

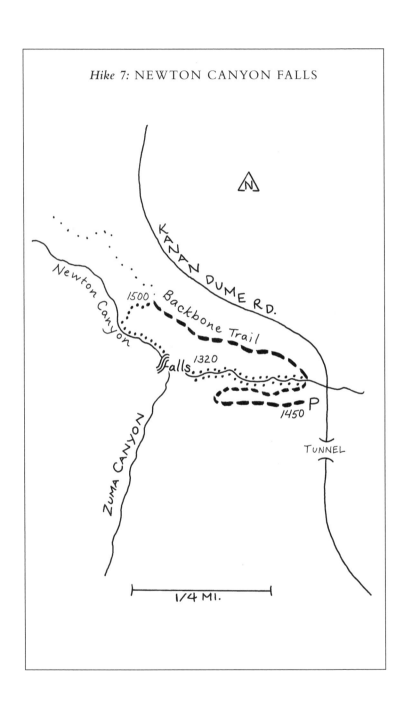

Hike 7: NEWTON CANYON FALLS

N

KANAN DUME RD.

Newton Canyon

1500

Backbone Trail

1320

Falls

1450

P

ZUMA CANYON

TUNNEL

1/4 MI.

❧NEWTON CANYON FALLS
Level 1, Hike 7

A trek through an overgrown playground hideaway to the top of the falls, and an alternate hike up the Backbone Trail, then down into the canyon beyond to the base

DISTANCE: 3.5 miles total: .75 miles to the top, 1 mile farther to base; one way and back; Elevation change: 250 feet

DURATION: 1–2 hours

NOTES: Dawn–dusk; dogs on leash permitted

DRIVING DIRECTIONS: Take PCH north to a right on traffic-lighted Kanan Dume Road. Directly after passing through a tunnel a few miles beyond, turn left into the large dirt lot at mile marker 9.5, where there is a sign for this as-yet unfinished section of the Backbone Trail. You can also take a south exit from the 101 Freeway on Kanan Road, which you'll follow to this point, and turn right into the parking lot; no fee.

Not so much a hike as a thorough exploration of a peaceful, hidden kingdom, this two-armed trek around Newton Canyon is a playful pastime romp. Begin on the trail at the rear of the parking lot, which quickly descends from sunlight into shade as it hairpins right down into the canyon. After a glimpse of the shady recesses of the upper canyon, the Backbone Trail crosses the creek and continues up the opposite side through leggy chamise, parallel to Kanan Dune Road. Continue along the trail until the point at which it bends left, away from the road, about a mile from the stream crossing. All along this part of the trail, barely noticeable footpaths, some with precipitous drops into rocky grottoes, lead down to the creekbed.

As you reach the bend in the Backbone Trail, a few more easily navigable paths to the stream lead down into the canyon. The base of the falls, which do no more than trickle down their thirty-foot cascade except following the strongest of rains, but instead offer a refreshing, leafy retreat from the city, can be reached by boulder-hopping and sometimes wading upstream about 250 yards. You can also do the same going downstream, the trail getting more rugged as you go, about the same distance to another dropoff point where Newton joins Zuma Canyon. Footing and balance are of paramount importance in both areas.

To get to the top of the falls, whose approach is far more serene and romantic than the one to the base, retrace your steps on the Backbone Trail to where it crosses the creek, then head straight down the creekbed, boulder-hopping and puddle-jumping, sometimes getting your feet wet. You make your way through thick vegetation to reach a string of intricate, rocky pool areas festooned in cattails, grasses, and moss, while brightly colored finches flit between adjoining oak and wild lilac canopies. A little shy of three-quarters of a mile, you reach the top of the falls, bordered by rocks that can be carefully navigated but are completely unstable, slippery, and dangerous near the center, even when they look dry.

On the way back, you marvel at the way the canyon, like all trails and paths, looks completely different than it did on the way down. Stop in one of the private miniglens on the bank for a secluded picnic or nap. Once revived by the relaxing spell cast by this cool, cozy canyon, turn right at the trail-crossing, and uphill, bearing left, to your car.

✤ PARAMOUNT RANCH
Level 1, Hike 8

A lively figure-eight plus sidetrips through the meadows, woodlands, grasslands, creeks, and movie-set ruins of this popular, still-utilized 326-acre film location

DISTANCE: 3.4 miles total; many shorter hikes possible;
Elevation change: 110–230 feet
DURATION: 1.25–2.5 hours
NOTES: 8 A.M.–dusk; dogs on leash permitted

DRIVING DIRECTIONS: Take Kanan Rd. exit south from the 101 freeway, bear left after .8 mi.—you will cross the large Agoura Road intersection—on Cornell Way, which immediately bears right as Cornell Road. Three miles farther on, turn right into the signed, dirt road entrance to the grounds on Paramount Ranch Road. Drive to the first crossroads, turn left, and park at the ranger's station down the road, where there are phones, restrooms, and picnic tables; no fee.

The directions above are quickest, but my favorite way to get to Paramount Ranch is by way of Malibou Lake, a secluded, little-known (even to locals) reservoir surrounded by the charming rustic estates of a private community and dotted with pleasure boats. For this alternate approach, exit the 101 south on Kanan Road, turn left on Mulholland Highway, go over the bridge, and soon after turn right on Lake Vista Drive, which abuts Cornell Road as it hits Mulholland again after scalloping down along the pictur-

Hike 8: PARAMOUNT RANCH

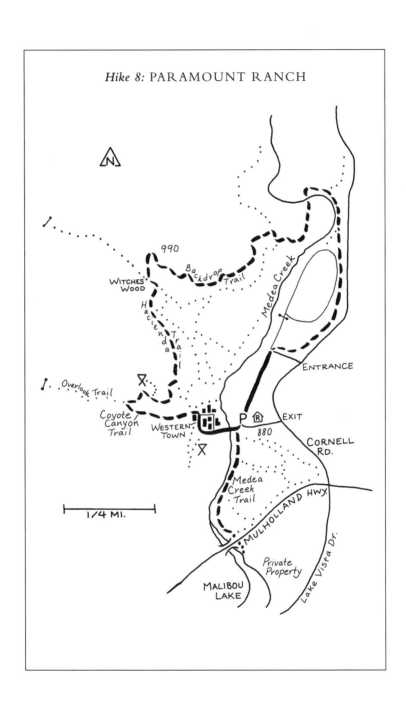

esque shores of Malibou Lake. From here, you'll turn left onto Paramount Ranch Road.

From the parking area, head toward the restrooms, then straight across the dirt road to a bridge crossing Medea Creek into Western Town, a little replica of a frontier village that has been used in countless movies and television shows. Wander through the town, with its equestrian park, saddlery, gunsmith, and mining equiptment [sic] store, to the train station—a large canopied platform featuring picnic tables.

Just behind the station is a sign reading COYOTE CANYON TRAIL. Follow it to your left, where white and yellow wild asters bloom year round, and a profusion of wildflowers can be viewed in the spring. At the first fork, the trail to your left leads you uphill to the border of the ranch for views of the mountains to the west. The Coyote Canyon Trail continues to your right, past a short spur hike up a hillock to a secluded, one-table picnic zone that you might be able to stake out if you come early enough on weekends, or on any weekday.

Heading downhill now, the Coyote Canyon Trail loops right back to the train station. You continue to your left, joining the Hacienda Trail, named for its use as a backdrop for movies with Southwestern or Latin-American settings. Continue to your right at the next fork, and up the hill to your left at the following one, circling the so-called "Witches' Wood," where fortune tellers set up their booths during the Renaissance Faires held at the Ranch during the 1970s. A sparse oak woodland that gets denser as you go, the Witches' Wood's main landmark is the burbling creekbed, where sticks perfect for divination and stones divine for scrying can be found. Curve around to your right over the creek; the trail straight ahead is another no-outlet trail to an overlook point at the boundary of the park.

Now on a wide gravel pathway, you see a trail rising up a hillock straight ahead of you. Go left up the fork and continue along the Backdrop Trail. The hills around you aren't marred by telephone or power lines or by any other sign of civilization, which is why this area was often used as a stock backdrop for geographical and historical wide shots. Continue straight at the next fork, then left at the next one toward the northern boundary of the park. There are trails crossing all over the place here, but it's almost impossible to get lost because there are easily reached vistas from which you can see most of the ranch. Continue going downhill through a field of scraggly mountain daisies, then curve right, and left, down toward the creek. At the northern boundary, where the creek curves west, cross it on the large sturdy planks provided, or explore its shady, overgrown banks for a while. The creek is gorgeous, with reeds and oak arching over it, though there can be a slight smell of sewage. Keep to your right as you cross through a gateway of two small boulders.

Keep in mind that you may run across a film crew doing their thing at any time here. It's okay to watch from afar, but don't, and especially don't let your children, get in the way of filming—it's a serious, time-constrained business, as you probably well know! Take your first fork to the right, which leads along the east side of the creek, then the left fork off the main road, which turns into a footpath leading along Cornell Road on the extreme eastern boundary of the park. Follow it to the park entrance, then right to the road you initially took to the ranger's station, all easily spottable here in a flat, scrubby expanse.

And if you can never get enough creekside exploring, continue past your car, past the restrooms, on the southerly Medea Creek Trail, to finish off your visit. Continue straight ahead at all forks, keeping along the creek, with many narrow trails leading down to leafy spots along its bed. This trail will take you all the way down under an overpass, where the creek flows into Malibou Lake. As you near the bridge, a tiny trail forks off to your right, taking you to a fence with a large, easily passable hole in it, to a lovely, sandy beach at the mouth of the lake, where you can snatch a few moments of serenity in no-man's-land. Pass quietly back through the hole in the fence, and retrace your steps to your car.

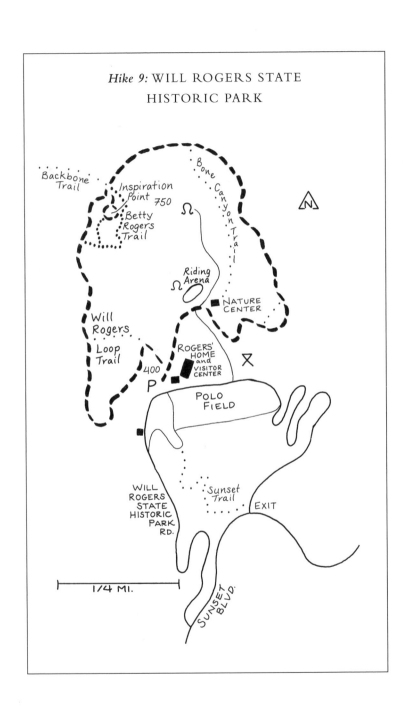

Hike 9: WILL ROGERS STATE
HISTORIC PARK

Backbone
Trail

Inspiration
Point 750

Betty
Rogers
Trail

Bone Canyon Trail

N

Riding
Arena

Nature
Center

Will
Rogers

Loop
Trail

ROGERS'
HOME
and
VISITOR
CENTER

400

P

POLO
FIELD

WILL
ROGERS
STATE
HISTORIC
PARK
RD.

Sunset
Trail

EXIT

1/4 MI.

SUNSET BLVD.

WILL ROGERS STATE HISTORIC PARK
Level 1, Hike 9

A nice climb to one of L.A.'s best Inspiration Points (there are many), and a pleasant descent to the wide green lawns of this welcoming palisades park

DISTANCE: 2-mile loop; Elevation change: 350 feet

DURATION: 45 minutes–1.5 hours

NOTES: 8 A.M.–5 P.M.; dogs on leash permitted

DRIVING DIRECTIONS: Take Sunset Boulevard west to the Pacific Palisades area, turn right on traffic-lighted Will Rogers Drive at the sign for Will Rogers State Historic Park, just past Amalfi Drive. The entrance is just under a mile up Will Rogers Drive. Park in the first, lower lot; $3 fee except very early in the morning (8–8:30) before the entrance station is manned.

The best place to start this charming minihike is at the far north end of the lower parking lot at the sign reading PARKING LOT SPUR TO INSPIRATION POINT LOOP TRAIL. Climb up the graded railroad tie stairs, following the white guard rail, and take a left at the first fork to loop down to the south boundary of the park. Continue up the west boundary on the wide trail through tall chaparral and eucalyptus, yielding to equestrians.

A few hundred yards up the steady hill, let yourself be enticed onto the Betty Rogers Trail, a small foot-traffic-only path leading to the right through arching manzanita, passing a couple of startlingly hidden glens as it forks to approach Inspiration Point from either side. Take either the short left spur straight to the point or the longer one straight ahead, with views of the riding arena and stables down to your right.

Inspiration Point is a bare hilltop studded with a large outcropping of boulders that you can circumnavigate. Views from here, when clear, are spectacular, and even on an overcast, late-fall or incipiently sunny winter day, the skyscrapers of Westwood, Century City, and downtown rise ominously blue and two-dimensional from the soupy white sky. You may be able to see for miles out to the sparkling green sea, or the view may be shrouded by dense layers of cloud. Either way, it is actually inspirational.

Once you've been inspired at the Point, head slightly north to rejoin the Loop Trail, bearing right past the left turn to the Backbone Trail. A few hundred yards from here, you can opt to take the hikers-only Bone Canyon Trail down past the roping arena to the nature center, or the longer, multi-use Loop Trail, which ends at the same destination.

Down the service road and across the lawn from here is the Will Rogers Home, with tours every hour on the half hour from 10:30 A.M. to 4:30 P.M. It remains decorated as the homily-spouter and his family arranged it for country weekends during the 1930s, but is hardly a historical monument. Your car is just past the restrooms and down the stairs by the payphones.

Picnics and barbecues are especially popular here on weekends, so if you're not directly involved in one yourself, come early, late, or on a weekday. Across from the main lawn and picnic area is

L.A. County's last surviving public outdoor polo field, where you can see local teams compete on spring weekends. Pick up an events calendar and one of the many humorous, informative pieces of literature available at the visitors' center should you want to know more about polo, Rogers, or the park.

Hike 10: MONROVIA CANYON FALLS

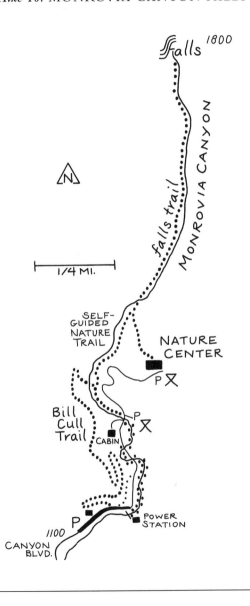

ꞈMONROVIA CANYON FALLS
Level 1, Hike 10

A pleasant, varied trail through one of the lushest canyons in the area to a tranquil waterfall, with plenty of creekside exploring available, and great picnicking

DISTANCE: 3.4 miles total: 1.7 miles to falls and back with minor alternate trails; Elevation change: 750 feet
DURATION: 1.25–2.5 hours
NOTES: 8 A.M.–5 P.M.; closed Tuesday; dogs on leash permitted

DRIVING DIRECTIONS: From L.A., take the 210 Freeway east to Myrtle Avenue, exit north, continue through downtown Monrovia (a charming old town), turn right on Foothill Boulevard; four blocks to a right on Canyon Boulevard. After three miles on Canyon, bear right at two soft intersections and follow the signs to Monrovia Canyon County Park. For the full tour, park at the small bottom lot near the entrance station; $3 fee. There are also further parking lots, picnic areas, and a visitors' center up the road nearer the falls.

Monrovia Canyon Park is green and inviting. Its lovely two-tiered waterfall is pleasantly reached by a rolling creekside trail, teeming with tourists, many in large groups, on weekends. Go on a week-day to avoid crowds.

The crowds are the only negative thing about the park. Its staff is friendly and forthcoming, its nature center rife with information about local flora and fauna, and its trails well-maintained. We're going to go on a full tour of the park here, including an adventurous trek down the creekbed on the way back from the falls.

Begin just past the entrance station, where the small, foot-traffic-only Bill Cull trail begins on a hairpin steeply up to the left. You hairpin right at the top of the hill, heading through a wild mix of chaparral and riparian plant life, then out toward the creek, where you bear left, and wend down with a few more turns across a couple of small tributaries through lusher and lusher vegetation. At the bottom of the canyon you cross the creek on stepping stones and turn left to join the main trail to the falls. To your right, or up any number of steep hillside blazer's trails, is the large picnic area and a walk across a high-canopied pine and oak woodland to the nature center.

Continuing up the Falls Trail, you wander along a rich riparian wilderness before crossing the creek and rising to the other side to follow the canyon wall, dipping to its floor now and then to any number of tiny trails down to the creek. Just before the falls you reach a rocky area providing alternate boulder-hopping routes to the spacious but cozy chamber where the forty-foot waterfall splashes over its two-tiered stage to a rocky pool below. The rangers are quite adamant about not climbing the walls of the falls, as several injuries and at least one death have occurred at this slippery site. Natural, multilevel smooth rock and log seating is available for prolonged viewing of this elegant, year-round waterfall.

For added adventure on the way back—and because the creek bears so many hidden wonders on its islets and in its thickets—stone-hop and ford your way right down its bed once you pass the series of impassable cement dams at the top of the canyon. Here you'll get a real sense of trailblazing, though you're never so far from the main trail that you can't yell out for assistance should you require it. The creek can be navigated, with some difficulty near the end, all the way to a small powerhouse with a steel bridge that blocks further exploration. Climb up the bank to your right here and turn left on the access road back to your car. And take a picnic!

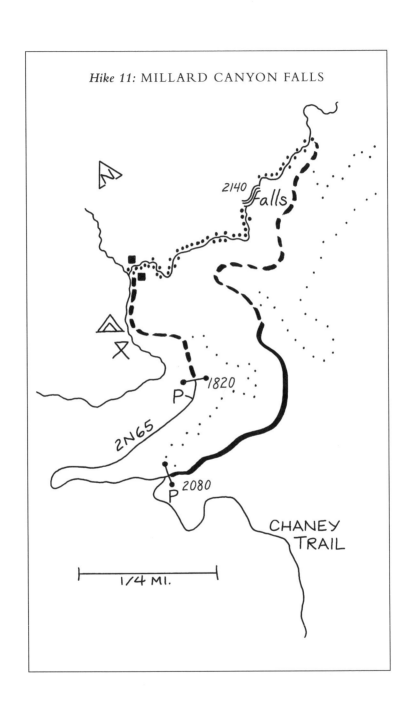

Hike 11: MILLARD CANYON FALLS

2140 Falls

1820
P

2N65

2080
P

CHANEY
TRAIL

1/4 MI.

MILLARD CANYON FALLS

Level 1, Hike 11

Two fun and easy routes to this cool, rocky canyon and its hidden waterfall—a short-creek hop to the base, and a longer hike to the leafy grotto at the top of the falls

DISTANCE: 3.7 miles total: .75 miles to base and back; 1.1 miles to top and back; Elevation change: 450 feet
DURATION: 1.5–2.5 hours
NOTES: 6 A.M.–10 P.M.; dogs on leash permitted

DRIVING DIRECTIONS: Take the 210 Freeway to exit north on Lake Boulevard in Altadena, just east of Pasadena. Follow Lake to its terminus to turn left on Loma Alta Drive, then right on Chaney Trail, to its terminus. The hike to the top of the falls begins at the locked gate to your right—park on the street. The trail to the base begins from the campground lot at the end of Road 2N65, a sharp turn downhill to your left; no fee.

We're going to start at the top here and work our way down. To reach the top of the falls, hook a right where Chaney Trail ends and start your hike past the locked gate on the connector road to the Sunset Ridge Trail. On your right, there's an interpretive map of the Mt. Lowe Railway and the hiking trails in the area, which will be explored later (Level 4, Hike 47).

Continuing up the road, you curve left and skirt high above the lush canyon. You may spot tents in the campground among the pines and oaks far below. You circle another arm of the canyon with sharp rock walls to your right. After several minutes you see the Sunset Ridge Trail forking off to your right; continue to your left down into the canyon, crossing a small, creaking metal bridge past a little brown cabin on your right. Nearly immediately, you descend directly into the canyon, with the main trail leading to the right through the creekbed, and a little trail to your left branching off down the canyon to the top of the falls. At the top of the falls is a daunting collage of boulders that filter water through their gaps. There are plenty of rustic picnicking possibilities here among alder-shaded pools and cascades. During the dry season, when the falls create an ambient sixty-foot spray, rather than a forceful rush, to their boulder-strewn base below, you can climb all the way to their edge and peer at people in the grotto below, which is where we're headed next.

Retrace your steps back to the locked gate at the end of Chaney Trail, get in your car, and drive down the 2N65, branching left at the end of Chaney Trail, to the large campground parking lot. Take the path at the canyon end of the lot to join with the dirt continuation of the access road. This leads easily through the campground and its attendant buildings. Soon after these, the Falls Trail splits off to your right for a half mile of easy creekbed hiking with a number of fun crossings and cascades all the way. You continue through a slight maze of rocks and a beautiful dappled grove of white alders on an engaging trail just challenging enough to make kids and beginners feel the rush of hiking adventure. The trail dead-ends at the base of the falls, where there is an impassable confluence of boulders blocking direct access. Sheer walls rise cathedral-like above you while you are misted by a cool spray. Here, and all along the trail, are numerous perfect sites for peaceful picnics. Simply retrace your steps to the campground, turn left on the campground road, and stroll back to your car.

⚘ STURTEVANT FALLS
Level 1, Hike 12

*A steep wander down into a wondrous canyon dotted with rustic cab-
ins to the almost theatrical setting at the base of the falls, and a steady climb
back up*

DISTANCE: 3.5 miles; partially looped near start/finish;
Elevation change: 700 feet
DURATION: 1.25–2.5 hours
NOTES: 6 A.M.–10 P.M.; dogs on leash permitted

DRIVING DIRECTIONS: Take the 210 Freeway east from L.A. to
Arcadia, exit north at Santa Anita Avenue, and take it all the way up
to its gated terminus, steep and winding for the last couple of
miles, at Chantry Flat, where there are three large parking lots, a
ranger's station, and dozens of widely spaced picnic tables;
National Forest Adventure Pass required.

Once parked, continue on Santa Anita Road past the locked pipe
gate to begin this journey through one of the quirkiest, most beautiful canyons in the Los Angeles area. Around the second bend of
the road, look to your right for the sign to the First Water Trail,
which branches off steeply down to the canyon below on a series
of switchbacks. Once in the canyon, under the dappled light
thrown by a mixture of alder, oak, and spruce, turn left on the trail
and head upstream. The peacefulness in this green, quiet canyon
makes it seem far more removed from the city than it is. This
serenity, along with the leap of the falls, draws hordes of visitors on

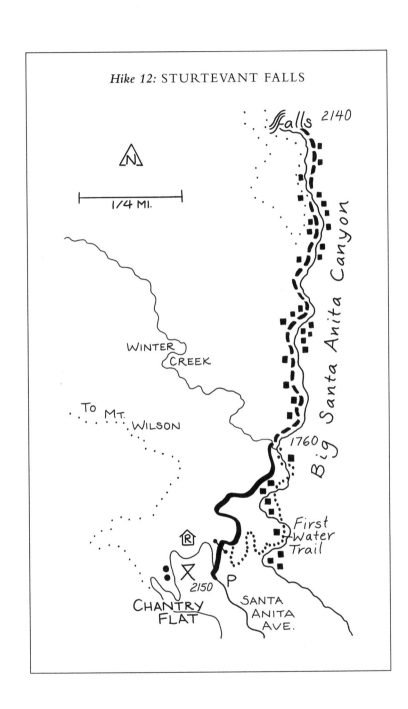

Hike 12: STURTEVANT FALLS

N

1/4 MI.

Falls 2140

Big Santa Anita Canyon

WINTER
CREEK

TO MT.
WILSON

1760

First
Water
Trail

R

2150

P

CHANTRY
FLAT

SANTA
ANITA
AVE.

clement weekends. I prefer the place on a weekday afternoon, especially when it's overcast and rich with complicated colors that pop in the subdued light.

Continuing upstream on the widening trail, you pass the place where Santa Anita Road junctions from the left—an alternate way down if the First Water Trail feels too steep for you. Immediately past this junction you see the first of over seventy rustic cabins, each decidedly different and equally charming, that stud the canyon all the way up to the falls—the remnants of an early wilderness camp for hikers. Now the cabins are used by their lucky owners mainly as weekend retreats, and often go up for sale. They can be had for a song, as they have no access to utilities and are not insurable for fire or other natural disasters, but they're darn cute, and one hasn't burned down for years!

You pass a point where the Upper Falls and Gabrielino Trails split off to the left as you near the falls, with half a mile of pleasant hiking to go before reaching the real show, where a sixty-foot cascade of water shoots through intensely chiseled borders. The soaring canopy of oak, alder, spruce, redwood, and cedar complete the dramatic effect.

To get back, you have two options: Hike the Sturtevant Falls Trail all the way back down to the First Water Trail and make a short but truly grueling ascent up its switchbacks, or turn right on Santa Anita Road where it branches off halfway down the canyon. After passing through a confluence of trails in a cool oak woodland, this seemingly innocent road heads quite steeply up itself, and doesn't level off until you reach the parking lot, which makes it not as difficult, but no less grueling, than the climb up the First Water Trail. The canyon and the falls are both well worth the slog.

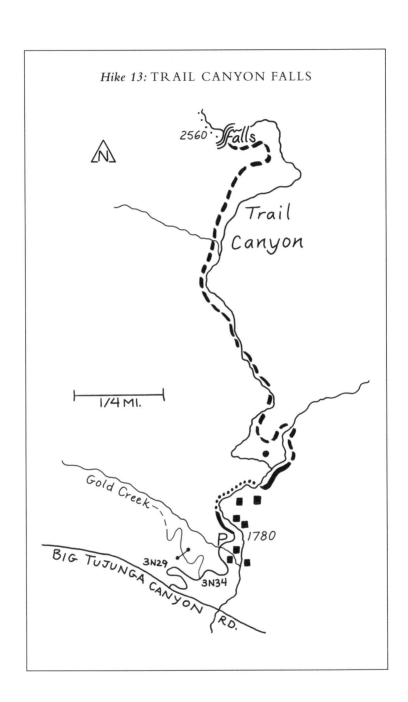

Hike 13: TRAIL CANYON FALLS

2560'

Falls

Trail
Canyon

N

1/4 MI.

Gold Creek

P 1780

3N29
3N34

BIG TUJUNGA CANYON RD.

☙ TRAIL CANYON FALLS
Level 1, Hike 13

A rugged canyon climb through rocky lower high country to this impressive waterfall, its wildly chiseled stage a sight in itself even when dry in late summer

DISTANCE: 3 miles; 1.5 miles one way and back; Elevation change: 700 feet

DURATION: 1–2 hours

NOTES: Dawn–dusk; dogs on leash permitted

DRIVING DIRECTIONS: From L.A., take the 210 Freeway west toward Sunland, exit north on Honolulu Avenue, bear right immediately after onto Tujunga Canyon Boulevard; turn left just over a mile later at the major intersection of Foothill Boulevard; 3 miles to a right on Mt. Gleason Avenue; over 2 miles with many stops to a right on Big Tujunga Canyon Road. Just over five miles later, start looking closely for a sign on the left for Gold Creek, and turn left on the signed, graded dirt road 3N29 here. Bear right on the 3N34 for Trail Canyon, and park in the large dirt lot at the end of the road; no fee.

The creekside and canyon wall trail to this majestic waterfall, impressive even when dry and breathtaking after heavy rains, begins past the locked yellow gate to your far left as you enter the parking area. After about fifty yards, you split off to the left on a foot trail that bypasses a few lazy curves in the road. It thrusts you into a dense, overgrown high country canyon, brown trail markers leading the way. You merge with the dirt road again after about a quarter of a mile, turning left, with a stone-lined border damming the creek to your left, then uphill, the overgrown canyon inviting you to visit via various sidetrails.

You continue on the road as it rises up through the canyon, then dips down into it, becoming a foot trail, with remnants of pavement. There is a lovely overlook spot just off to your left as the road curves down and to the right again. You see an incongruous TV antenna just in front of you at a hairpin left down earnestly into the canyon. The trail splits off the road here according to the brown sign that leads you down across the creek, which is wild and narrow with sheer walls on either side. Copses of white alder actively dapple and fray what little light there is even at day's end. Sycamore and oak begin to mix with alder and spruce as you cross the creek several times.

Soon you climb out of the creekbed and backtrack to a narrow trail that leads steeply up the canyon wall. You climb earnestly as the canyon falls below you to your right. The trail begins to even out as the canyon and trail both take an abrupt left just before the site of the falls. You can see them down in the canyon between two large clefts of granite. There's a little trail that leads off right to the edge of the falls where you can sit on a rocky promontory and watch and listen to the falls splashing below you after rains. There's also a much steeper trail down to the base of the falls, but it is extremely slippery and dangerous, and difficult to get back up. Try it only if you are an expert or a daredevil. The rugged rocks here at the top are an excellent place for meditation. Simply retrace your steps back to the parking area.

LEVEL 2:

Learning Loops, Canyons, and Strands

Demanding and involving but not difficult; appropriate for novices and older children; these are unhurried pleasure trips or sturdy workouts for the seasoned hiker.

⚘LOWER FRANKLIN CANYON
Level 2, Hike 14

A rugged climb to a vista point overlooking upper Beverly Hills, and a shady, interesting nature trail in this citybound canyon park laced with paths

DISTANCE: 3.8-mile loop; Elevation change: 440 feet
DURATION: 1.25–2 hours
NOTES: Dawn–dusk; dogs on leash permitted

DRIVING DIRECTIONS: From Sunset Boulevard, turn north on Beverly Drive; turn left, continuing on Beverly Drive at first intersection, and left again where there is a fire station to the right; jog left around the triangular dog park, and turn right on Franklin Canyon Drive. You will pass a Santa Monica Mountains Conservancy Parkland sign and a gate heading into the park. At the first intersection after entering the park you come to a little white house with a red-tiled roof to your right. Turn a hairpin right here onto Lake Drive and park in the small dirt lot to your left at the sign for the Franklin Canyon Ranch and Hastain Trail; no fee.

The wide, well-tramped Hastain Trail, always populated with local upscale joggers and dogwalkers, curves steadily uphill from its signed starting point at the far end of the small parking lot through a rocky, mountainous landscape choked with hardy chaparral. One great thing about this canyon is that there are literally dozens of trails going every which way into strange, rugged territory. You could have some wild and woolly in-town exploration on this

Hike 14: LOWER FRANKLIN CANYON

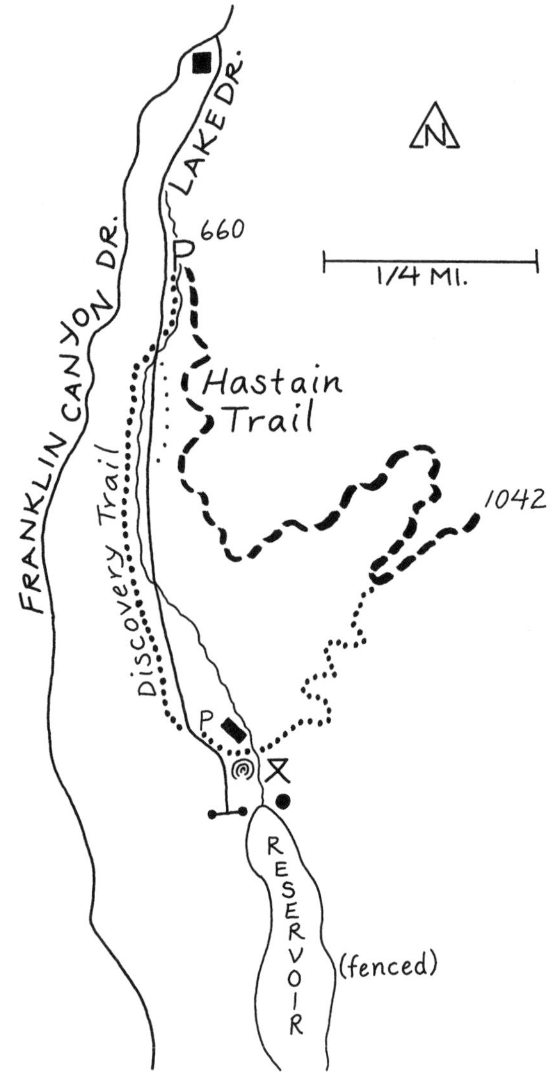

LAKE DR.

FRANKLIN CANYON DR.

Discovery Trail

660

Hastain
Trail

1042

N

1/4 MI.

P

RESERVOIR

(fenced)

wayward web of tiny, sometimes imperceptible trails, but we'll stick to the main trails in this hike. Wear long pants here as the chaparral on the small trails is extremely prickly, and the lower main trails are laced with poison oak.

Continuing up the Hastain Trail, you pass a big beekeeping concern with its whitewashed boxy hives to the left. Near the apex of the trail at just over 900 feet, you reach a trilevel boulder formation where the trail curves uphill slightly farther to 944 feet at a lookout point featuring a pile of boulders ringed in chamise. To your right, a narrower trail leads down to the grassy park below. Return to this point after reaching the zenith, and take this trail, indicated by both the boulder formation and a sign with a picture of a bicycle on it.

This winding trail is steep as it bleeds into the riparian lushness of the creek below, but pleasantly shady and less crowded than the Hastain Trail. At its end you find yourself in a large grassy park with picnic areas, private residences, and an amphitheater. Walk across the lawn to the far corner near the parking lot, cross the street, and pick up the Discovery Trail, which hugs the opposite wall of the canyon along Lake Drive back to your car. As it descends into the creekbed, this lush, ferny trail is a thrill for adventurous small children, with its profusion of morning glories and lilies tangling about the feet of huge, gnarled oaks and sycamores, one in particular spreading like a banyan, just waiting to be climbed.

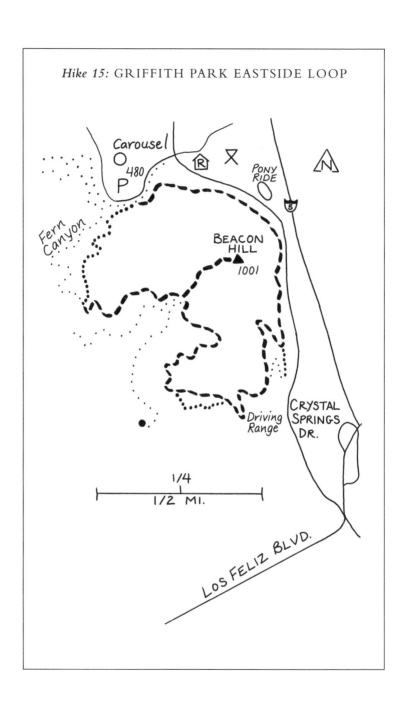

Hike 15: GRIFFITH PARK EASTSIDE LOOP

Carousel
480
P
Ⓡ
Pony Ride
Fern Canyon
N
5
Beacon Hill
1001
Crystal Springs Dr.
Driving Range
1/4
1/2 MI.
Los Feliz Blvd.

⚹ GRIFFITH PARK EASTSIDE LOOP
Level 2, Hike 15

A rambling climb through Fern Canyon on large and small trails to Beacon Hill, and a stroll around its base above the eastern border of this wild, 4,200-acre park

DISTANCE: 5-mile loop; Elevation change: 600 feet
DURATION: 1.5–3 hours
NOTES: 6 A.M.–10 P.M.; dogs on leash permitted

DRIVING DIRECTIONS: Turn north on Crystal Springs Drive into Griffith Park from Los Feliz Boulevard just west of I-5. Head past the main parking section, around a big curve past the pony rides and ranger station, and turn left at a complicated intersection where you see the sign for Merry-Go-Round Parking. Park to your right in the huge lot, which is very crowded on weekends; no fee; carousel rides are $1.

Listen to the crazy, muffled calliope of the carousel as you start your hike and head into the woods. Begin by walking back out of the parking lot, cross the street toward a NO BICYCLES ALLOWED sign. A wide bridle path leads uphill here, with a fork almost immediately. Take the right fork, leading up to a smaller foot trail that bypasses the lazy looping of the wide Fern Canyon Trail to the top of the hill above you. You can go the longer way, which is less strenuous, by turning right just across the street, going up a few yards on the path, and making the first left, where you will see a wooden arch welcoming you to Fern Canyon.

On the steeper, more secluded path to the upper trails, odd footing problems and wacky twists and turns keep you alert through a tangle of scrub oak and scrubby pines. Here you get a taste of what most of Griffith Park is like: Too steep to develop, which makes it, at five times the size of New York's Central Park, not only the largest city park, but the greatest expanse of untouched, citybound nature anywhere.

After a short but intense climb you come to a main dirt road, the Fern Canyon Trail, on which you turn left. You see the Griffith Park golf courses, Burbank, and Glendale below you. After a couple of wide turns you come to a five-way hub in the road. Up to the left is a spur trail to the top of Beacon Hill—a short, steady climb to some great views. Back at the hub, take the trail leading straight across the intersection from the one upon which you initially arrived. It heads slightly downhill, where you make a lazy horseshoe around a nearly vertical, overgrown canyon. You look down upon the freeway and the Tregnan Golf Academy amid the thick canopy.

Just after completing the head of the horseshoe around the canyon you come to a fork. Take the trail uphill to your right, which ends under a power pylon reading 450 in a yellow diamond. At this point, find fabulous views of downtown by peeking through the oaks before you or hiking just a bit up the spur trail to your right. To the left, a small trail leads down under the power lines. Take it, and shortly you come to another larger trail. Here you swing a left around a sharp hairpin, go right past the driving range, and at the next fork, instead of going down to your right, continue up to your left. You hairpin beneath Beacon Hill heading toward Crystal Springs Drive and the freeway, with magnificent views of Atwater, Glendale, and Downtown. At the top of the next hairpin there's a little trail leading up to a thicket on the top of the hill, which is an interesting hiding place. This is the type of foot-path that crisscrosses all over Griffith Park, cutting off from the main, graded multi-use trails.

Sticking to the main trail, hairpin to your left, and head down-hill above the freeway. Passing closely under Beacon Hill to your left, you may be able to make out the odd trails of the few brave souls who have actually tried to scale the peak from this side. Climb again as you curve away from the freeway, coming to a vista of the northeast side of the park. You might see the red-and-white awning of the carousel nestled among the trees below you. Soon you are back at the initial intersection from which you took off uphill on the Fern Canyon cutoff, with the parking lot down to your right.

Hike 16: MALIBU LAGOON
AND CARBON BEACH

CROSS CREEK RD.

Malibu Lagoon

PACIFIC COAST HWY.

Malibu Point

Malibu Lagoon State Beach Museum

PIER

CARBON BEACH

Pacific Ocean

1/4

1/2 MI.

⚘MALIBU LAGOON
AND CARBON BEACH
Level 2, Hike 16

A short circuit through the Malibu Lagoon area and a long walk down a narrow, beautiful stretch of Malibu Beach

DISTANCE: 5 miles; mostly one way and back on the beach; Elevation change is negligible
DURATION: 1.5–3 hours

DRIVING DIRECTIONS: Take PCH north to traffic-lighted Cross Creek Road, turn left into the Malibu State Beach parking lot; $3 fee.

A small trail on the south side of the parking lot leads to a lagoon, where many trails and hideaways beckon. Soon you find yourself lost in a maze of sea grass, stumbling across recently used vagrants' hideouts, some choked with trash. After finding a little muddy promontory that looks out across the lagoon with its attendant string of brown pelicans, you follow the maze back to the parking lot, where schoolchildren have taken over if it's a weekday morning.

You head across the lawn, briefly visiting the information boards in the central kiosk, across the main bridge toward the beach into a tranquil wildlife sanctuary. Pelicans, ducks, egrets, herons, mud hens, and various turtles make this their home; explore it on any number of miniature side trails to your left. Turn left when you hit the strand, going south along the little sandspit that separates lagoon from sea. This sheltered, wave-producing crescent is where all the baby and preteen Malibu surfers come to hone their skills, and beyond it is one of the best and moodiest stretches of beach in Southern California. Include a walk on the pier if you like, then pass under it, heading south down the narrow beach past the mismatched chorus line of sea shanties and beach mansions, most with head-high Plexiglas walls to keep the high tide from their manicured gardens. The beach itself is public, though many threatening signs will try to convince you otherwise, and walkable only during low tide. Consult your local weather report for tide time coordinates.

A brisk, forty-five-minute jaunt down this driftwood-strewn strand brings you to a closely set cove of rocks in front of a fanciful house dressed in cobblestone and sporting a miniature widow's walk, where you can practice boulder-hopping, provided you're well aware of the slipperiness of rocks that appear only at low tide. A few minutes farther along, a sheer-walled promontory precludes further progress. Turn around and head back. If you're a celebrity-miner, this is one of the richest quarries on the coast, and since you know enough to walk at low tide, they'll assume you must be a local just taking a constitutional from your beachfront manor. Act nonchalant, and do it barefoot, no matter what the season.

⚘CHARMLEE NATURAL AREA
Level 2, Hike 17

A ramble through the grasslands, oak woodlands, and rich coastal scrub of this 460-acre park, with amazing ocean views and profuse spring wild-flowers

DISTANCE: 4 miles total: intricate 3.5-mile loop; .5 miles one way and back ocean view; Elevation change: 600 feet
DURATION: 1.25–2.5 hours
NOTES: 8 A.M.–sunset; dogs on leash permitted

DRIVING DIRECTIONS: Take PCH north to Encinal Canyon Road, turn right, continue five miles to a left turn at a wide turn-out with a callbox where there is a large sign for the park. Park in the first dirt lot to your right; $3 fee weekends and holidays only.

This seaside bluff is one of the best places in Los Angeles to view spring wildflowers. On this intricate loop you'll visit ocean views, oak woodlands, and meadows, with some rugged climbing up and over chaparral-choked in-between zones. To begin, head through the gate on the paved road, pass a small picnic site, and bear right up toward the nature center—you can pick up a map here, or at the kiosk at the turn in the road. On the way, you pass the Russell Butterfly Garden; the nature center, open only on weekends and holidays, is to your left.

You go uphill and switch an extreme left at the top, where the road goes from paved to dirt, and head toward a water tower in the distance. Wonderful views of mountains surround you. Follow

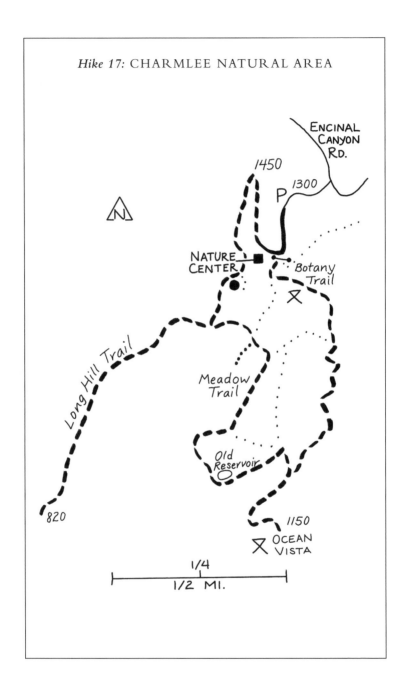

Hike 17: CHARMLEE NATURAL AREA

ENCINAL
CANYON
RD.

1450

1300

P

N

NATURE
CENTER

Botany
Trail

Long Hill Trail

Meadow
Trail

Old
Reservoir

820

1150

OCEAN
VISTA

1/4

1/2 MI.

the main road, forking right at the spur to the water tower. You soon come to another fork, where you turn left, going slightly up, then downhill. For a solitary sidetrip, even when the park is crowded, which it usually is on weekends, turn right here and take the steady climb up the aptly named Long Hill Trail to a secluded ocean vista among high chaparral and rock formations.

Heading left at the intersection, the trail narrows and cuts through oak, sage, and other chaparral scrub. You pass under a great shady oak and head uphill to a crossroads. Here you might be enticed to take the trail to the right, leading to a lovely stand of oak studding a small bouldered plateau—another secluded hideaway just minutes off the main trails. From the crossroads follow straight through with the trail you were initially on, which descends into grasslands and curves right to cross the large meadow that is the heart of this parkland.

Having crossed the meadow you soon come to a wide fork. Going up to the right will offer you an amazing view of the ocean below, including surf and thousands of miles of foreshortened sea, or you can go all the way to the little hillock you see topped with manzanita, to your right, as a tiny sidetrip. The main trail curves to your left here; you soon rise to an open space with more ocean views, surrounded by old eucalyptus trees. On your left is a large, long-unused cement water cistern sunk into the earth. Skirt the cistern on its right, using its perimeter as your trail for a bit, then continue on the wide dirt trail past some cattails and more eucalyptus.

After rising and falling you come to another fork in the road. Curve down on the right fork, then left through overgrown chaparral. To your right is a small spur trail to the best ocean view in the park, surprisingly uncrowded most of the time, featuring peaceful picnic table areas. Far below, maroon kelp colonies dot the ocean's turquoise surface.

Follow the main trail away from the sea, down through a slight gorge of overgrown chaparral, then swing up to your left past an interesting Swiss cheese–like sandstone formation toward another bunch of oaks. Bear right at the T-intersection toward some denser oaks just below you. You pass through a small oak savannah with plenty of shade, huge, sturdy trees to climb, and an abundance of flat, soft spaces for picnicking or napping.

This woodland goes on for quite a while as you skirt it to your right with a meadow to your left, and then fades to bristly chaparral, with manzanita trees sticking menacingly out from the tops of sage clusters. Another lovely clump of huge shady oaks awaits you in a few minutes, this one particularly spacious. Head uphill from here to another small gorge lined with sage, manzanita, and toyon, then descend into a cool, shady ecosystem of reeds, oak, mesquite, and plenty of poison oak.

You are now on the (unmarked) Botany Trail. This is the loveliest, shadiest part of the whole park, well worth a lazy dally or a picnic, either in a secluded glen or at the large oak-shaded picnic area to your right as you near the wide, main access road on which you started your hike. Turn right here, and head directly down past the gate to your car.

⚘DEVIL AND YBARRA CANYONS
Level 2, Hike 18

An exciting trek through an enchanted riparian wilderness, overgrown in parts, wide and shady in others, and bejeweled with biomorphic sandstone formations

DISTANCE: 5.4 miles: 2.7 miles one way and back; Elevation change: 500 feet mostly rolling
DURATION: 1.75–3.5 hours
NOTES: Dawn–dusk; dogs on leash permitted

DRIVING DIRECTIONS: Take the 118 Freeway west to Topanga Canyon Boulevard, exit north, where Topanga Canyon Boulevard terminates; turn immediately left onto Poema Place, and park on the street; no fee.

The origin of Devil Canyon's name is obscure, but perhaps it came from the rounded, yet surprisingly angular, sandstone formations that jut into the canyon like Day of the Dead masks throughout much of this lush, cricket-serenaded hike. You begin on an unused paved road to your north, at the terminus of Topanga Canyon Boulevard. Keep to the right of the giant boulders in the clearing where the road turns to dirt and descends into the canyon.

In the 1930s and '40s there was a paved road all the way through the canyon, but it has long since been taken over by nature. The asphalt soon ends, dry scars of it appearing here and there along the trail. Down in the creekbed, this hike can get muddy even in the dry summer and early autumn, and it is a posi-

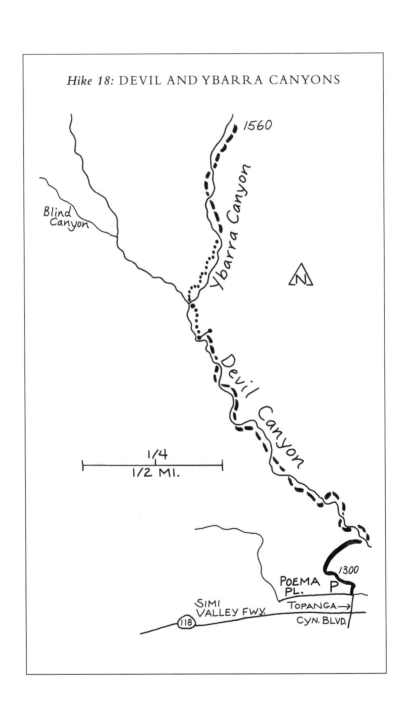

Hike 18: DEVIL AND YBARRA CANYONS

1560

Ybarra Canyon

Blind Canyon

N

Devil Canyon

1/4
1/2 MI.

POEMA
PL.   P   1300

SIMI
VALLEY FWY.   TOPANGA →

118   CYN. BLVD.

tively sole-sucking slog after rains, though the solitude and scenery in the narrows are worth every puddle. You cross the creek many times, chancing now and then upon small caves hidden by vines, or tiny overgrown tributaries. Continue through the bed when the trail seems to disappear: It will pick up again before you can become too panicked that you might be going the wrong way.

Soon you are rewarded with a steep, riparian oak savannah, riddled with poison oak. You continue along the creek to pass a small pipe fence, which you might want to use as your turning-back point if the wilder canyon beyond daunts you in the least.

Beyond the fence the trail becomes more rugged, leaves the canyon for a bit, bears right at a fork where small, overgrown Blind Canyon leads off to the left, climbs an arid, chaparral-laden rise, and wends back down into an even more overgrown canyon, where you follow a nerve cluster of trails under small bays and alders. This tricky trail becomes more manageable after a while, then dips down across the creek to carry you to the east side of it, on the old road again, which takes you on a short rise out of the canyon and into the sunlight once more. Meadows appear to your left, and signs of equestrian travel dot the widening trail, which continues up and out of the canyon to join a tangle of roads to the arc of radio tower peaks and look out points high above you in the Oat Mountain area. This is your official turning-back point, though you may continue as far as you wish before tracing your trail back to civilization.

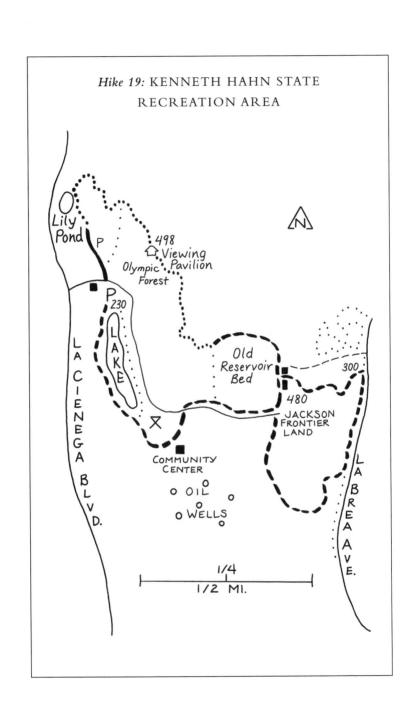

Hike 19: KENNETH HAHN STATE
RECREATION AREA

Lily
Pond

P

498
Viewing
Pavilion

Olympic
Forest

P 230

L
A
K
E

Old
Reservoir
Bed

300

480

JACKSON
FRONTIER
LAND

L
A
C
I
E
N
E
G
A
B
L
V
D.

COMMUNITY
CENTER

OIL
WELLS

L
A
B
R
E
A
A
V
E.

1/4
1/2 MI.

N

⚹ KENNETH HAHN STATE RECREATION AREA
Level 2, Hike 19

A walk through a much-loved local park, a trek through its dusty chaparral and oil field borders, and a hike to a series of ridgetop terraces with 360° views of L.A.

DISTANCE: 4.5 mile figure eight; Elevation change: 450 feet

DURATION: 1.5–3 hours

NOTES: 8 A.M.–sunset; dogs on leash permitted

DRIVING DIRECTIONS: From I-10, take La Cienega Boulevard south, cross Rodeo Road, turn left at the signed park entrance, and park in the first lot to your right near the small, landscaped lake past the entrance station; no fee.

Head toward the lake first on this intermittently intense ramble through a well-designed park that has been plagued by fire, and greenly proclaims its powerful place from the oil fields and busy streets that surround it. It's a nice little lake, surrounded by laconic locals fishing or quietly steering radio-controlled mini-yachts, which tend to excite the already nervous ducks.

After passing the lake on one of its well-maintained dirt trails or walkways, head left to pass the community center, where you cross to the left side of the street and continue on the sidewalk up the eucalyptus-lined hill to a recreation area dubbed Jackson's

Frontier Land. This playground and picnic plateau overlooks a steep chaparral wilderness, bordered on the east by busy La Brea Avenue—one of the main arteries to LAX. Pass between the rest rooms and the radio towers toward two yellow poles. Just before these, take the trail leading down to the right. There are numbered posts here correlating to a brochure for a native plant series, but the community center is often out of the maps.

After winding down a chaparral-choked canyon finger, you come to a viewpoint overlooking La Brea Avenue, from which you can see all of Mid-Wilshire, Downtown, and Hollywood. You soon descend to a T-intersection next to the busy thoroughfare, where the La Brea Green Belt Connector Trail takes over. To your left is a paved service road; beyond it lies a wild and confusing crisscross of hillside trails, on which I have often found myself looking into someone's backyard without the least idea of how to get back to the Green Belt, though La Brea Avenue is visible, and sometimes noisy, just below. You could wander for hours here, and never get out, especially if you fall into one of the many shallow sinkholes covered by foliage.

If this adventure doesn't pique your interest, you need only turn right at the T-intersection for the Green Belt Connector Trail. This leads you up into an eerie oilfield wasteland across some burnt-out meadowland.

You soon loop back toward Jackson's Frontier Land, where you pass the radio towers again, and go straight onto the trail that leads along the drained reservoir around which the park was built. The grassy slopes into the smooth bowl of the empty reservoir are ideal for rolling down. Instead of going all the way around, take the small foot trail leading down at the northwest corner, which hugs a wall above the planted area of the park below. The trail winds along the canyon wall to a series of overlooks outfitted with benches and pavilions. At the last overlook, take one of the several trails leading down to your left to the northern outskirts of the park. A stairway takes you down to a strolling path through a garden and pond area with some of the biggest lily pads you'll ever see. Your car is in the lot across the street past the entrance station.

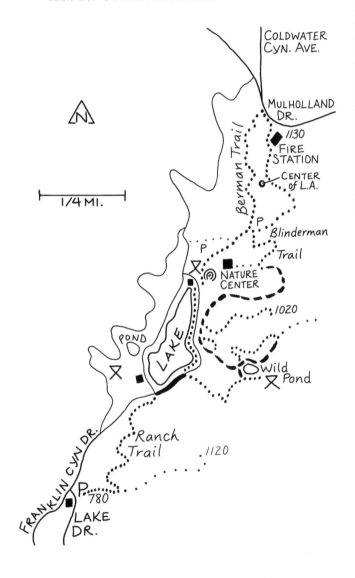

Hike 20: UPPER FRANKLIN CANYON

COLDWATER CYN. AVE.

MULHOLLAND DR.

Berman Trail

1130
FIRE STATION

CENTER of L.A.

P
Blinderman
Trail

P
NATURE CENTER

1020

POND

LAKE

Wild Pond

Ranch Trail
1120

FRANKLIN CYN. DR.

P 780

LAKE DR.

N

1/4 MI.

⚘UPPER FRANKLIN CANYON
Level 2, Hike 20

An intricate, Chinese box of a loop through the charming upper reaches of this hilly, citybound canyon, including the geographical center of L.A. and a lovely lake

DISTANCE: 5-mile crazy loop; Elevation change: 600 feet
DURATION: 1.5–3 hours
NOTES: Dawn–dusk; dogs on leash permitted

DRIVING DIRECTIONS: From Sunset Boulevard turn north on Beverly Drive; turn left, continuing on Beverly Drive at first intersection, and left again where there is a fire station to the right; jog left around the triangular dog park, and turn right on Franklin Canyon Drive. You will pass a Santa Monica Mountains Conservancy Parkland sign and a gate heading into the park. At the first intersection after entering the park you come to a little white house with a red tiled roof to your right. Bear right and head straight across Lake Drive to the small dirt parking area right before you, with a rustic bridge and hillside staircase beyond it; no fee.

From your parking space, go directly across the bridge and steeply up the stairwell along a creekside hill. The canyon here is overgrown and lush, a tiny jungle in the middle of L.A. At the top of the stairwell you make a sharp hairpin left to stay on the main trail. If you go straight up, the trail becomes an ever-narrower footpath that ascends a steep hill leading to the abandoned foundations of a housing development at the top of the canyon, with sliding or bushwhacking the only ways back down. So turn left at the hairpin at the top of the creekside stairs, and continue on the Ranch Trail toward the upper canyon lake.

After ten or fifteen minutes of casual winding along this lovely trail you find yourself at Franklin Canyon Drive. The lake is below you. You follow the road around the first curve to the right, past a speed limit and NO PARKING sign, with a small picnic area to your left. Straight ahead of you in the next parking area you spot another trailhead. Take the trail straight ahead just past the DO NOT LEAVE VALUABLES IN YOUR CAR sign. Climb straight up through a grove of eucalyptus, then downhill to a fork where you turn right to the Wild Pond. Head right around it to a picnic table and grape arbor, where the trail used to go through to the other side of the pond, but has been overgrown by grape vines. There are many little canyons down here to explore.

Backtrack from here to the fork you came to at the bottom of the hill, and turn right (taking the left fork if you're going to skip the pond). Almost immediately you come to a very wide trail, on which you turn right. As you turn the corner to the left along a gulley, you see several trails leading off to your right, festooned with wild grapes and papyrus. Step over the gulley here, and take the graded wood-tie steps up to your left. The trail you were on continues up a steep hill here to the brambly outskirts of a hillside housing development.

The hillside trail onto which you have climbed loops around back down to the crossroads at the bottom of the hill. As you descend back to the Wild Pond crossroads, turn right. Shortly thereafter you come to Franklin Canyon Road again, where you turn right, uphill onto another trail leading up another wood-tie staircase. This hike is an effective and scenic alternative to the boring StairMaster. Just before a bench on the right, you see a righthand turnoff—a recommended sidetrip up to a hilltop overlooking the whole canyon. A quick five minutes up will give you a full view of the lake below and the mountains, with their many precarious cliffside glamour dwellings, above.

Turn right back down on the main trail, and continue uphill and to your right as you near the road. You swing around, cross a bridge, and hit a graded dirt road. Turn left on this road; just as you come to a fenced-in shed area you see another trail heading up to your right. Turn right and go back uphill along another set of railroad-tie stairs. Below, you can see part of the Santa Monica Mountains Conservancy Project at work, reseeding new plants and growing saplings before working them back into their natural habitats. This trail heads downhill behind the Sookie Goldman Nature Center, which is geared toward entertaining children with basic nature information. They host more children's events here than almost anywhere else in the city.

Passing a barbed-wire fence as you head toward a parking lot and gate, you come to another small fork in the road, where you turn right on your way to the Center of L.A. Pass through a parking lot, across a wooden bridge, and take a sharp right uphill at the next crossroads. The brown post that you pass on your left on your way to the fluttering windsock above you on this rather steep climb is the geographical center of L.A., and the building you reach at the top of the trail is a Fire Department Safehouse, Station #108. Walk straight across the helipad, keeping to your left, toward Coldwater Canyon Boulevard, and turn left on the trail leading down back into the canyon off the near side of the street beside the guard rails.

This trail sticks to your left as you descend into the canyon, past two dry cement runoff barrier walls. Winding down into the canyon, then back up and down again, you find yourself back at the parking lot from which you initially reached the geographical center of Los Angeles. Head down and straight through the parking lot, sticking to your left. At the small rise past the gated grate and the yellow water hydrant, you may hear the old eucalyptus tree squeaking and creaking in the wind behind you. Continue straight at the fork, and at the next fork, with the parking lot to your right, stick to your right through the grassy picnic area. You soon reach the road that leads around the lake; bear left on it. On your left you'll pass the Tongva Kicha, a replica of an indigenous Santa Monica Mountains housing and storage unit.

At the ONE WAY sign, you see a place to your right where you can climb over the short wall along the lake, and take a trail leading down to its shores. The trail runs down through the boulder-laden surge basin, bears left, and then circles the east side of the lake back to Franklin Canyon Road. On the other side of the lake there are picnic areas, a small redwood grove, and farther down, on the other side of the street, a tiny nature trail with a manmade pond as its centerpiece.

You walk along the shores of the lake to its south bank, and cross Franklin Canyon Road. Straight ahead of you are the stairs back up to the Ranch Trail, on which you started. Follow this trail back to the leafy canyon in which you began your hike, then take a sharp right down the steep stairs, and at the bottom cross the bridge over which your car awaits.

⚘PORTER RANCH LOOP
Level 2, Hike 21

*A variegated loop through the hidden wilds and wild suburbia of the
north valley, including Aliso and Limekiln Canyons*

DISTANCE: 5.6-mile loop; Elevation change: 700 feet
DURATION: 1.75–3.25 hours
NOTES: Dawn–dusk; dogs on leash permitted

DRIVING DIRECTIONS: From the 101 Freeway take the Balboa
exit north all the way through the valley to a left (west) on Rinaldi
Avenue. Park on the street just after crossing Zelzah Avenue, where
you see a street sign for "Hesperia" on your right leading to a dirt-
road dead end and broken-down white fence; no fee.

Slightly farther west on Rinaldi is a trail leading down on the
west side of Aliso Canyon Creek, where you begin your multi-
environmental loop through the newest excrescences of the San
Fernando Valley suburban stronghold.

As this trail leads you to its first crossing of the creek, you spot
a slightly overgrown fork to the left, and take it. It leads through a
sometimes blinding grassland on the outskirts of the canyon near
the wall. A bit of bushwhacking takes you to a trail laced with
morning glories; it's evidently much-loved by equestrians. As you
near the neighborhood above, you spur around a gate onto a paved
road, and then climb a sharp left up the hill as the trail continues,
nearly straight into a set of tennis courts. Beyond this you cross

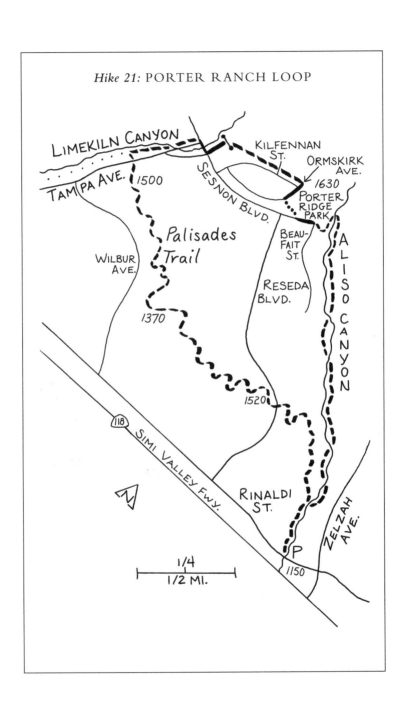

Hike 21: PORTER RANCH LOOP

LIMEKILN CANYON

KILFENNAN ST.

ORMSKIRK AVE.

TAMPA AVE. 1500

SESNON BLVD.

1630

PORTER RIDGE PARK

Palisades Trail

BEAU-FAIT ST.

WILBUR AVE.

RESEDA BLVD.

A L I S O   C A N Y O N

1370

1520

118

SIMI VALLEY FWY.

N

RINALDI ST.

ZELZAH AVE.

P

1150

1/4
1/2 MI.

Reseda Boulevard, and continue on the now-marked Palisades Trail, which follows Reseda for a bit then goes off up to the left.

The Palisades Trail winds around the wall of the canyon above the well-manicured suburbs below you, bordered by an attractive fence made of split telephone poles. After this it descends directly behind a series of backyard pools and up over a saddle, where you cross Tampa Avenue into Limekiln Canyon. To your left, the canyon winds down to Rinaldi street 1.5 miles to the south. Turn right on the partially paved trail, and head up Limekiln Canyon to Sesnon Trail and Porter Ridge. Scramble down to the creek if you can for paradisical settings well worth the difficult access.

After a few minutes you come to a fork littered with confusing signs. Ignore them, and continue on your far left into the shade. Go straight across a never-finished dead-end paving into a shady glen; after a few more minutes you cross Sesnon Road. Ahead of you is a gas company entrance, which you skirt to your right to Tampa Avenue, turning left to follow it a hundred yards to its terminus. Proceed toward the END sign. Just to the left of this obvious warning you see a more demure sign that announces STREAM WATER NOT FOR DRINKING, and a paved trail leading back behind the neighborhood to your right. Pass the end of a dead-end street, onto the dirt trail that leads behind backyard pools into which you are most assuredly dying to jump if you've attempted this trip during the hot, dry summer.

As you come to another dead end street, you see a sign that reads SESNON TRAIL TO LIMEKILN CANYON, and very faintly registered beneath this, an arrow pointing to Aliso Canyon, straight down. Turn right on this street, named Ormskirk, past Kilfenan, and down across Porter Ridge Park to Sesnon. Take a left to the dead end at Beaufait, which leads you back to Aliso Canyon. Go

past the yellow gate, and wind down the hill to the canyon, curving sharply southeast and then straight ahead to your car. This is a
lovely, often shady walk through a hardy, oak-dominated riparian
wilderness, its dust kicked and settled by a constant parade of
horses, its roots challenged by a thick, enterprising web of moist
morning glories.

✤ GRIFFITH PARK CENTRAL
Level 2, Hike 22

A variegated, rambling loop with some challenging spells through some of the major attractions of Griffith Park, with outstanding views of the L.A. Basin

DISTANCE: 6-mile loop; Elevation change: 1,125 feet
DURATION: 2–3.5 hours
NOTES: 6 A.M.–10 P.M.; dogs on leash permitted

DRIVING DIRECTIONS: From the 101 Freeway, take the Western Avenue exit north to the end of Western as it blends east into Los Feliz Boulevard. At the first light turn left onto Ferndell Drive. Park along the street near the point where Black Oak Drive branches off and the fenced Fern Dell area begins to your left; no fee.

This is my favorite Griffith Park hike, utilizing a variety of interesting trails and footpaths. You begin at the corner of Black Oak, through the gate to exotically planted Fern Dell, where over 300 species of fern mingle and bicker in a tightly landscaped creekside wilderness. Meander through this wonderland, then swing right under a small bridge before exiting through a gate. Bear right up the hill past the bathrooms, just above and to the right of the stream. You soon connect with a wider trail that rises high above the canyon toward the observatory. As you pass directly under the white dome of the observatory you can either scramble up the side of the hill to the next tier, or go more gently around the wide curve to your left.

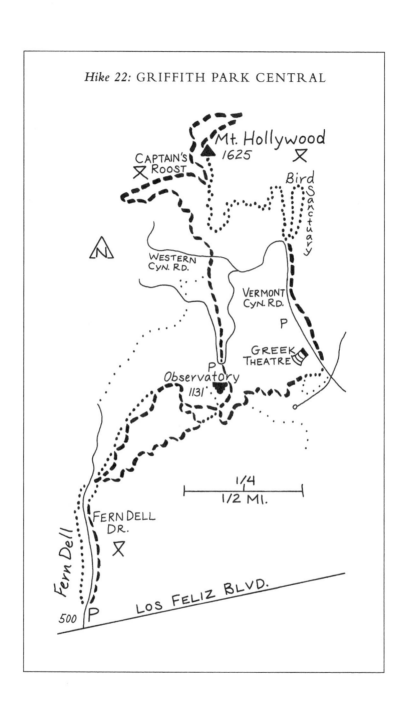

Hike 22: GRIFFITH PARK CENTRAL

Mt. Hollywood
1625

CAPTAIN'S ROOST

Bird Sanctuary

WESTERN CYN. RD.

VERMONT CYN. RD.

P

GREEK THEATRE

P

Observatory
1131

Fern Dell

FERN DELL DR.

500 P

LOS FELIZ BLVD.

1/4
1/2 MI.

At a crossroads directly south of the observatory, take the lower right fork, which soon merges with an abandoned street. Follow it down to the right. A few yards in, the trail picks up again to your left. As you head down toward Vermont Canyon Avenue, you come to a place where the trail takes a sharp hairpin to the right. Just ahead, there's a narrow gulley trail that avoids the lazy curves of the road; take it if you like hill scrambling.

You end up right below the Greek Amphitheater at the corner of Commonwealth Avenue and Vermont Canyon Road. Turn left up Vermont Canyon Road past the Greek. As you near the out-skirts of the theater parking lot, the street curves to the left. To your right is a bird sanctuary with a tranquil loop trail through a cool well-treed haven seemingly devoid of aviary life. It's a nice place to sit and think. Take the short loop through this wilderness, and make a hairpin right uphill where there's a beat-up old green sign reading "29" in white near the street.

This trail leads up above the sanctuary, then curves left, and right again, on its sometimes precarious way to Mt. Hollywood, which soon appears straight ahead of you to the north. Down to your left you see a lacing of fire roads, which you'll be taking on your way down from Mt. Hollywood to the observatory. There are a number of trails leading up to Mt. Hollywood from a six-point crossroads right below it. I prefer the gulley trail leading straight up the mountainside to its bald pate, studded with picnic tables. This is a particularly strenuous route, so you might choose to take the winding fire road to your left.

From the top of Mt. Hollywood, take the trail past the solar panel to the north, and at your first opportunity take the sharpest left possible back downhill. Fork left at the green water tower reading "151." A bit farther down, you come to one of my favorite picnic and resting areas in the park—a many-tiered, well-planted hillside with a plaque reading IN LOVING MEMORY OF JOE GOLDMAN, 1901–78. HE LIKED THIS PARK. This charming plateau is called the Captain's Roost. Below it, you reach the same crossroads you hit just before climbing Mt. Hollywood. Make a sharp right and head down the hill on the long switchback to Mt. Hollywood Drive.

Soon you come to a bridge that crosses Western Canyon Drive. The trail going down to your right is the Mt. Hollywood Trail, which is uninspiring. Instead, climb up the central trail, or the smaller ridge trail to the left, both of which take you to the observatory parking lot. Go straight toward the observatory and observe. See the planetarium; gaze at the awesome views of the city from the terraces.

As you head back out, face the observatory and find the trail leading down about thirty yards in front of the building to the left, with a small sign reading "21." A few minutes down this trail you come to a familiar crossroads; take the shallow right down the hill, heading west to a fork where the road you took up earlier comes up the hill on a hairpin to the left. You continue straight, or north. As you come to a sharp left down the hill, you see right in front of you a tree with some silver graffiti on it, and a small, not-well-traveled trail leading down the hill into a wilderness beside it. After a short descent on this hidden footpath, you cross the road again. Either join it or continue on the footpath all the way down the hill to the little pond garden just outside Fern Dell. Head through the dell, or along the grassy park to your left, back to your car.

✿ MARSHALL CANYON MEANDER
Level 2, Hike 23

A delightful figure-eight loop through the best parts of two shady, capacious canyons and across a lower San Gabriel ridge featuring panoramic views on all sides

> **DISTANCE:** 5.5-mile figure eight; Elevation change: 1,000 feet
> **DURATION:** 2–3.5 hours
> **NOTES:** Dawn–dusk; dogs on leash permitted

DRIVING DIRECTIONS: Take the 201 Freeway east to where it blends into the 30 Freeway east, to where that merges with Foothill Boulevard east. Turn left (north) at the major intersection of Wheeler Road, then right on Golden Hills Road. Before Golden Hills curves right, turn left onto Stephens Ranch Road. Past the golf course, the road curves right; pass a fire station to your left; just after this is a right turn into a large, signed "Multiple Use Trail" dirt parking lot. Park at the far end near the picnic area; no fee.

Start at the MARSHALL CANYON TRAIL sign on the east side of the parking lot, next to a small picnic area. Bear downhill and to the right out of the parking lot's southeast corner to begin this varied hike through two amazingly unspoiled canyons. You begin by curving down a sandy hill on a large equestrian trail to the junction between Marshall Canyon and Live Oak Canyon.

Soon you are smothered in the shade of oaks and the chirping of crickets. You gingerly explore the creek during this first dip to

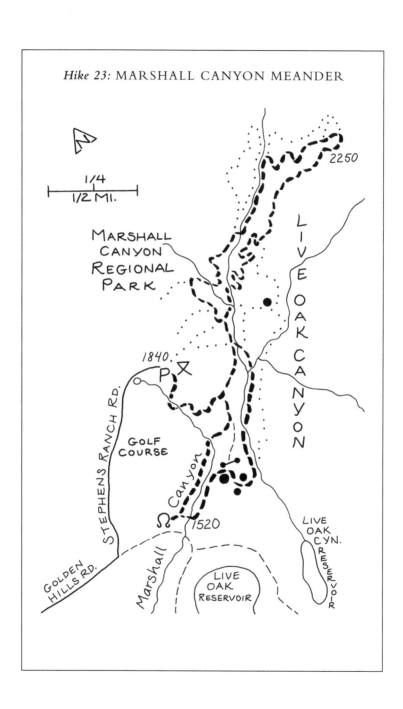

Hike 23: MARSHALL CANYON MEANDER

its banks, and soon rise out of its bed again. After about fifteen minutes you come to a T-intersection facing a multitiered rock formation. Turn left to dip through the canyon, then back up to your left. You climb up and pass through a large dirt lot. To your left a fenced gravel parking lot borders what looks like a little kids' pony ride, with a park beyond it. Continue straight through on the trail. As the main trail turns left along the chainlink fence you see a few somewhat trodden footpaths, if a bit daunting, down to the canyon floor below you to your right, which is incredibly shady and lush even in the summer, and riddled with poison oak.

After twenty to thirty-five minutes you come to a three-way fork. Head straight through on the middle fork. At this point you descend into the capacious canyon, full of spindly, twisted oaks, sycamores, and all sorts of vines, with plenty of ways to explore the creekbed below. This is an easily walkable trail for families, and rife with hidden romantic spots. Soon you come to another T-intersection, where you turn right, though the sign for the Marshall Canyon Trail tells you to turn left. Every single trail in the canyon, in fact, is called the Marshall Canyon Trail.

You continue in the shade and cool of the canyon. In a few more minutes you come to another fork, where the large trail curves off and back the way you came. Take the smaller trail to the left that shoots off farther into the canyon. It hairpins quickly up to your right, then left again, keeping a steady climb, to several points with wonderful views of the oak, alder, and sycamore canopy below you. You're soon high up in the chamise-tufted hills to the east of the canyon, on a very steady uphill climb with even better views to come. Off to the southwest you see Live Oak Reservoir like a postage stamp in the distance. On the final, steep leg, the trail shoots up abruptly to the east and takes you all the way up to the top of the hills, where it looks like some subdividing was started years ago, though it's mostly grown in now.

Keep climbing toward the bald apex, staying left on the main trail as you hit a fork near the top. As you can see in front of you, the trail bounces along the ridge, slightly more uphill, and then down into a saddle between two hilltops, where, to your left, you see a sign reading MARSHALL CANYON TRAIL—as they all do. Here you turn left and descend. Again, you dip quickly into shade, and soon find yourself hairpinning down into the canyon, this time with pines and eucalypti mixing in with the oaks and sycamores.

You follow the creek for a while, and see another trail apparent on the opposite bank, then after a while dip down to cross the creek and join up with a spur that leads out to a wide, multi-use trail. Turn left, continuing down the peaceful, spacious canyon. This hike is all about the ups and downs of rolling hills and the chiaroscuro of shade and light. It's deserted and tranquil even on weekends, though you may pass riders in the lower reaches of the canyons.

The trail rises above the canyon to settle into a saddle with a bunch of signs, all of them reading—you guessed it—MARSHALL CANYON TRAIL. Turn left here, at the sawed-off telephone pole next to a large oak tree. Twenty yards beyond that, the road will veer off to the right, and the smaller trail will lead down into the canyon to the left. The trails here are like a paper cutout snowflake gently laid over a completely wild and undeveloped network of canyons.

Keep to your left as a fork leads sharply to your right back uphill. Just beyond this you see another large intersection. Head straight through it, keeping to the right. You wander back through the shady canyon, and as you begin to rise up toward the fence, dip down to your left to continue on to Live Oak Canyon, the lower half of our figure eight. This is one of the loveliest parts of the hike; the creekbed is very easy to reach, and there are several interesting rock formations along the hilly route. If you want to go farther, or turn a different way, note that all trails are connected.

The angles of sunbeams through spindly alders are spectacular here, refracting light off leaves in a sharp crisscrossing web. Softer shafts of sun sweep down through the openings in the tangled oaks, which beg to be climbed upon (especially those growing in arches over the trail). You go by a little bridge on your left that looks exactly like the one the Three Billy Goats Gruff might have hidden under, onto a rarely used fire road. The trail curves around and heads uphill. There is a baby water tower on your left and a mama water tower on your right, encircled by barbed wire along a row of eucalypti. Beyond you is a geodesic dome structure, also surrounded by barbed wire. You skirt the large water tower, bearing right, and then left down into the canyon again between two small chain-link barriers for a runoff system, before you get to the chained steel-pipe gate/telephone pole fence that leads off on to a wide ridgetop access road.

After ten to fifteen minutes you come to a three-way intersection. The trail to your left goes right up to the stables where you can rent horses. Carry on straight over the creek and bear right to head back up through Marshall Canyon. Enjoy the peace here, especially if you get stuck behind a slow-moving gang of neophyte riders. A short rise up from the canyon will bring you to a familiar spot—the boulder formation outpost where you initially descended from your spur leading from the parking lot above. Turn left here for a brief uphill jaunt back to your car.

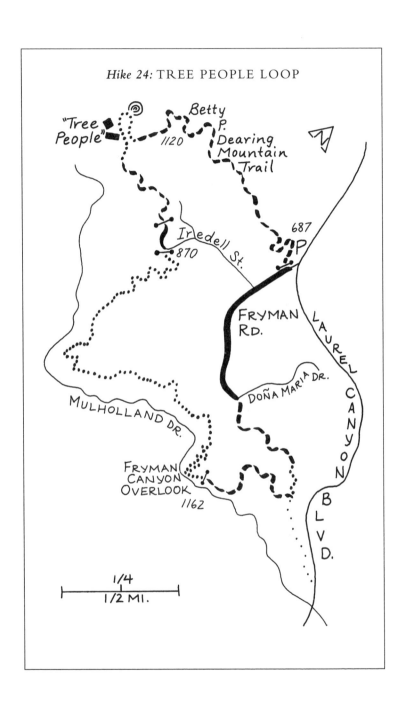

Hike 24: TREE PEOPLE LOOP

"Tree People"

Betty
P.
Dearing
Mountain
Trail

1120

687
P

Iredell St.

870

FRYMAN
RD.

Doña Maria Dr.

L
A
U
R
E
L

C
A
N
Y
O
N

MULHOLLAND DR.

FRYMAN
CANYON
OVERLOOK

1162

B
L
V
D.

1/4
1/2 MI.

⤴ TREE PEOPLE LOOP
Level 2, Hike 24

A multifaceted loop through Studio City's Wilacre Park to the home of the "Tree People," then through Fryman Canyon to a scenic overlook on the Betty Dearing Mountain Trail

DISTANCE: 6.4-mile loop; Elevation change: 700 feet
DURATION: 2–3.5 hours
NOTES: Dawn–dusk; dogs on leash permitted

DRIVING DIRECTIONS: From the 101 Freeway, take Laurel Canyon Boulevard exit south, pass Ventura Boulevard, and turn right on Fryman Road. Turn right again immediately and park in the spacious Wilacre Park parking lot; no fee.

This interesting, citybound loop utilizes the Betty P. Dearing Mountain Trail, the Fryman Canyon Trail, a series of connectors, and a couple of suburban streets to explore the steep interstitial wilds of wealthy hillside neighborhoods, with two short, sweet sidetrips. The signed Betty P. Dearing Mountain Trail begins beyond a gate beside the Wilacre Park administrative office near the entrance to the parking lot. You start out climbing up a nicely shaded paved walk through, perhaps, a flurry of local exercisers and dog walkers. Small foot trails cut off big loops of this winding trail. At the top, to your left are raised lots surrounded by overgrowth, copses, and thickets. You take a sharp left at the corner of an open field, and descend slightly to a big clearing featuring a box that reads AIR IS PART OF THE CITY FOREST.

This is the home of TreePeople, a nonprofit environmental organization dedicated to urban forest preservation and education (818-753-TREE). To your right, their nature trail, with plaques on trees dedicated to donors, makes a lovely sidetrip. Take one of the stone stairways up to your left, where you hit the headquarters, along with a recycling and education center. Here you can pick up various information about TreePeople and related events and agencies. Hairpin down on the upper tier of their nature trail back to the Dearing Mountain Trail, just beyond the point where you turned off.

Continuing on the trail, you pass a yellow gate after half a mile, and hook up with Iredell Street. Walk about fifty yards on the street and veer to the right onto a dirt road leading to another yellow gate. Swinging around the gate and climbing to the end of the chain-link fence, you find yourself on the decidedly less-used part of the trail; stay left at the fork. You begin a steep climb up a railroad-tied hillside, barbed wire here and there reminding you that you are on the border of the land of the privileged.

At the next fork there's a crossroads in a clearing from which you can see Mulholland Drive straight ahead of you under a radio tower. Turn left down the largest trail, walking parallel to Mulholland. Below you are a couple of villas, so close they're nearly touching, that really make you wonder why wealthy people insist on building right on top of each other. Start descending, turn right back toward Mulholland, and soon you reach a shady stand of willows that leads down into the coolness of Fryman Canyon to cross a creek that rushes blissfully during wet months. Bear left at the next fork, approaching a large eucalyptus glade with a bunch of old eucalypti fallen across the trail at a stream that runs down into an enticingly explorable riparian wilderness below.

As you exit this first stand of eucalypti, the trail seems to go on to another. Stop here and look closely for the almost graffitied-over sign reading DEARING MOUNTAIN TRAIL. Make a right and follow it up the hill to cross another small stream, then wind along right below Mulholland Drive. At a small clearing, take the right fork, heading southeast. Here the trail hairpins down into the canyon. In the shade again, you pass a piece of sculpture . . . no, wait, that's the rusted old hulk of a wrecked green-and-orange VW Thing. Take a few terraced steps down and cross another seasonal stream to the site of another wreck, possibly a red AMC Gremlin. Look behind you to see the treacherous curve on Mulholland Drive that might have accounted for these accidents. Take a right fork sidetrail to head uphill again through scrub oak and chamise, switchbacking to a big white gate introducing Fryman Canyon Overlook, a paved area with wooden steps up to a vista point from which you can examine the whole valley before you, and the mountains beyond.

Backtrack a short way on the Dearing Trail, and after a couple hundred feet you see the hairpin which you took up to the overlook. Head straight as it continues east below Mulholland Drive. You pass a huge hillside blanketed in mustard and anise, skirting the canyon to the east. At the first junction past a big pepper tree, you take the left fork down a trail cut between leggy anise, which covers you in a light perfume of licorice. At the bottom of this short, steep hill you reach a utility road where you turn left, peering through fences at inviting pools in the backyards to your right. You hit a big bank of bright pink oleanders as the dirt road turns to asphalt, and pass through your last yellow vehicle gate at the corner of Dona Maria and Fryman Road, which you follow three-quarters of a mile back to your car.

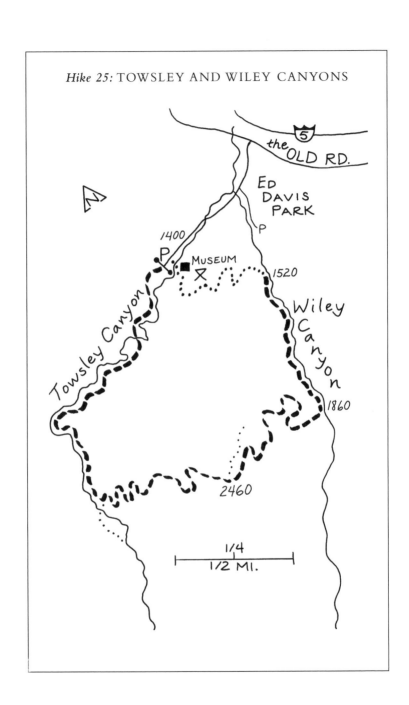

Hike 25: TOWSLEY AND WILEY CANYONS

the OLD RD.
5

ED DAVIS PARK

P

1400
P
MUSEUM
1520

Towsley Canyon

Wiley Canyon

1860

2460

1/4
1/2 MI.

༈ TOWSLEY AND WILEY CANYONS
Level 2, Hike 25

A country road and a ridgetop trail link two picturesque canyons in the Santa Susana Mountains, with miles of ever-developing valley to view from above

DISTANCE: 5.2-mile loop; Elevation change: 1320 feet
DURATION: 1.75–3.5 hours
NOTES: Dawn–dusk; dogs on leash permitted

DRIVING DIRECTIONS: Take I-5 north out of L.A. to Santa Clarita and exit at Calgrove Boulevard. Turn left, go southwest under the freeway to merge with The Old Road; half a mile to a right turn into Ed Davis Park at the large sign. Follow the dirt road past the first parking area; it gets a bit bumpy from here on out, but it's only a short drive to the next parking area, above and to the right where the road dead-ends at a chain and post fence. Park here, with the lawned park area and buildings across the road; no fee.

This was Chevron Oil land before 3000 acres were turned over to the Santa Monica Mountains Conservancy in the mid-nineties. Ed Davis Park now spans almost 4,000 acres of pristine, rugged wilderness, but Towsley Creek bubbles brown after rains with the exuberance of the still-active oil veins below the canyon floor. Your hike begins just beyond the chained gate down a wide, graded dirt road into Towsley Canyon. Almost immediately you're greeted by a large canopied oak to your left that can be climbed upon, with a lovely shady patch beneath it for napping and picnicking. You pass through another gate or go around it under the large California black walnut, which, along with the similar, but smaller, elderberry, dominates the tree population here in these twin canyons.

Crossing the creek, you continue along the main trail to your left as a narrow trail branches off down to the creek to your right—a worthwhile exploration. Trees become denser as the trail narrows, and you look up to see the sheer, complicated cliffs of the narrows ahead of you. Up to your right the jagged little hills of chaparral dance in the spring breezes or jitter in the summer sun. Unprepossessing at first, this trail becomes more and more beautiful as you walk along, also giving the feeling of greater and greater seclusion, with lots of hiding places here and there just off the trail, mostly among oaks or white alders.

Just under the beautiful cliff that you have been approaching, the trail makes an abrupt left into the narrows. The scenery becomes spectacular here as the walls of the canyon take you in their slim cradle. You tread right across the edge of the creek on the skirt of a cliff. Here you find water even in the dry season, and marvel at the odd conglomerate rock wall just above you to your left. It can be muddy through this gorgeous wild canyon. You cross the creek and hug the right wall for a bit, dipping down to cross again, and leaving to climb slightly to a wide open space where you get an astounding view of the lower reaches of the canyon. Take the Towsley View Trail, to your left at the TRAIL 13 marker. Towsley Canyon can be explored another half a mile from this point, with a number of secluded picnic or meditation zones to choose from.

The View Trail rises above the canyon through a large patch of small, graceful elderberry trees, then continues up for about a mile on a series of switchbacks as the foliage of narrow ravines tumble down at you. The trail levels out for a bit on a narrow hillside heading east, accompanied by heavy whiffs of sulphur from the chemical excretions of the land. You curve up and continue climbing through a series of shady oak woodlets until you reach the top of the hill; to the north you see the valley spread before you (with some very boring cookie cutter tracts scarring the western foothills).

You turn right at the edge of an oak savannah to climb up one more peak; if you need to rest there's a lovely place right before you turn right under an elegant pin oak. The last hill is very steep. At its apex you are rewarded with an even shadier copse of oak, and a viewing log on which you can sit to survey the valley below. The trail carries on steady for a bit with a lovely strip of hilltop oak savannah to your right, then dips down and back up a bit more through some tall manzanita, with views throughout, sticking high up just below a ridge to your right before reaching a fork. Take the right fork; the left one is actually just a little gulley. As you head downhill, catching some vast views to the north again, there's a trail out to the overlook you see far to your left—a worthwhile trip for view collectors, but unnecessarily strenuous for most who have already climbed so steeply.

Continue down to your right on your way to Wiley Canyon, below you to your left. The trail curves around an arm of the canyon as you near the bottom, getting wider as it descends onto the canyon floor, and finally depositing you at an opening marked by a brown post on its closest left corner. Turn left here, proceeding down the canyon on a shady trail next to the oily creek. After several minutes you see side trails off into more oak-shaded creekside rustic picnic areas. After twenty to thirty minutes you pass through another gate, rusted brown and perpetually open. Just past it, you turn left on the last leg of your journey, the signed Canyon

View Loop Trail, which takes you on long switchbacks up and over a small ridge, then gently down to the museum and park, with placards introducing native trees and plants along the way. The Sonya Thompson Nature Center, hidden among the trees of the ingeniously planted picnic grounds, is open only on weekends. Your car is just across the dirt road.

ꙮLOWER ZUMA CANYON
Level 2, Hike 26

A full tour of lower Zuma Canyon using a circuit of riparian, chaparral, grassland and coastal scrub trails, with some fine ocean views

DISTANCE: 5.2-mile loop; Elevation change: 1,100 feet
DURATION: 1.75–3.25 hours
NOTES: Dawn–dusk; dogs on leash permitted

DRIVING DIRECTIONS: Take PCH north to just south of Zuma Beach, turn right on Bonsall Drive, and continue at its terminus to the far end of a large dirt parking area; no fee.

This rambling, varied loop crisscrosses Zuma Canyon to rise high above either side of it, and allows you to explore the lower canyon to the outskirts of the dense and mysterious narrows, a demanding trek which you can take on in Level 4, Hike 48. Past the brown gate, you enter the wide lower wash of the canyon, with its dominant sycamores, sprinkling of oaks, runaway cultivated plants like oleander, and thick juicy vines such as morning glories. Grasses and papyrus tufts join leggy coastal wildflower scrub and diasporic poppy colonies to complete the perfect coastal canyon picture. After two-tenths of a mile, you turn left onto the Zuma Loop Trail, and right shortly after as the Zuma Ridge Trail climbs to the left. Be careful of the signs: Last time I was here they were pointing in the wrong direction. No matter what the sign says, turn right here to continue on the Zuma Loop Trail—the next sign you pass will reassure you.

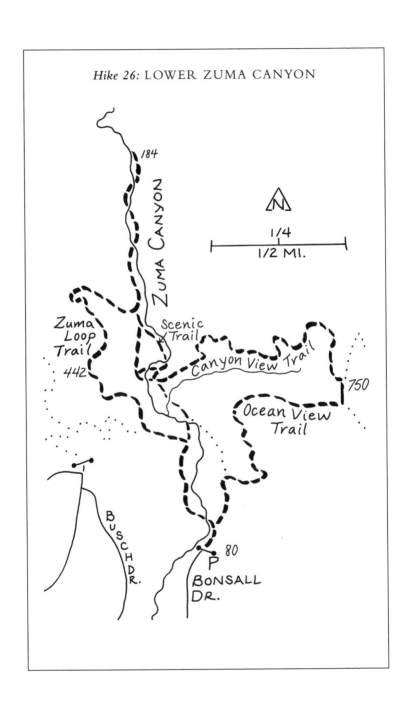

Hike 26: LOWER ZUMA CANYON

ZUMA CANYON

184

1/4
1/2 MI.

Zuma
Loop
Trail
442

Scenic
Trail

Canyon View Trail

Ocean View
Trail

750

BUSCH DR.

P
80

BONSALL
DR.

After a short trip through high chaparral and grasses you descend into shade near the canyon, where the trail hairpins right to rejoin the creekbed around a bend with a great three-pronged oak that is one of the best climbing trees around. These trails are used more by equestrians than hikers, so watch for droppings throughout.

Once down in the canyon, you turn left to explore the canyon for .7 miles, where the trail ends unceremoniously just past a ten-foot clump of anise at a sandy beachlet. All along the canyon, the creekbed is incredibly dry and sandy during the summer and fall, and can be both muddy and deep during wet times of year. From this point, the trail gets narrower and continues in its own way for a while. Retrace your steps to the sign at which you initially turned up into the canyon, and bear left through a wash to the next fork. For variety take the signed Scenic Trail to your left, which takes you along the south side of the canyon and rejoins the Canyon Trail.

Shortly after that, you curve to the left, and come to another fork where you head left onto the Canyon View Trail. You climb steadily and strenuously, switching back and forth to the ridge, where Zuma Beach appears before you. Down to your left, the small black snake of Kanan Dume Road slithers through the canyon. You head straight out toward the ocean, and turn right at the next fork onto the Ocean View Trail. Descending through scrappy fields that are profuse with wildflowers in early spring, you hit Zuma Canyon again in just over a mile. Cross the creek and turn left soon after on the Zuma Canyon Trail for a quick walk to the parking area.

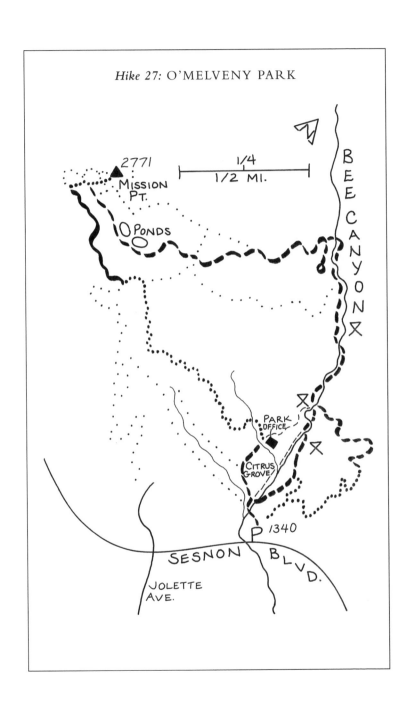

Hike 27: O'MELVENY PARK

⚘ O'MELVENY PARK
Level 2, Hike 27

A vigorous climb to the peak at Mission Point, and a wander through grasslands down into steep and fascinating Bee Canyon, plus a gorgeous lawned park

DISTANCE: 5.6-mile loop; Elevation change: 1,500 feet
DURATION: 2–3.5 hours
NOTES: Dawn–dusk; dogs on leash permitted

DRIVING DIRECTIONS: From the 101 Freeway, exit Balboa Boulevard north all the way through the valley. Pass Rinaldi and Joletta to turn left on Sesnon Avenue. Just after the road narrows, turn right into the well-signed parking lot for O'Melveny Park; no fee.

As you enter the park, you see a sign for the Nature Trail to your left along the orange and grapefruit grove. Ahead of you up the main access road are restrooms, park buildings, and acres of rolling picnic lawns under generous oaks. Near the buildings, there is a board that features a map of the area.

To begin this strenuous loop (that is a harbinger of even steeper climbs to come), cut left across the citrus grove, where you see another sign for the Nature Trail on your left. This is a nice little trail for kids that leads to a natural grotto in one of the outlying arms of Bee Canyon Creek. Continue to your right along the beige fence on the wide dirt trail. Cross the creek behind the park office, and as you reach a patch of grass with some oak trees to your right, take the smaller trail leading off to your left up into the hills and canyons. Here begins the long climb to Mission Point.

After rambling through some thick chaparral and crossing the stream, you start a steep ascent that leads you up quickly through the two arms of the creek on a high ridge between them. If you turn around there are fabulous views of the north valleys. Having climbed a thousand feet in under a mile, you come breathlessly to a T-intersection. Turn left, continuing uphill. In a very short while you hit a wide fire road on which you turn right, still continuing uphill. Stay on the fire road as a trail veers off to your right, or take it as a shortcut to a large crossroads near a fence, where you continue straight up through some richer shades of chaparral to an oak grove plateau, with lovely places for resting, and then straight up the even steeper hill in front of you along a series of gullies to the top of Mission Point, with its piled stone zenith marker. This, you find, is dedicated to Mario A. de Campos, MD, who was a mountain climber and loved this peak. On a clear day you can see forever from here.

Once you've talked to God or done whatever it is you like to do on top of mountains, go straight back down the way you came to the oak tree plateau, and then farther down to the large crossroads at the chain-link fence demarcating the boundary of O'Melveny Park. Take your first left before reaching the fire road, cutting through another opening in the fence. You pass a pond to your left that looks more like a ceremonial circle for some lost tribe in the dry season. There are sidetrails leading down to it. You go over a hump and start heading downhill through tall grasses, then hook a left as you begin your long, rambling descent into Bee Canyon.

Halfway down you pass a beautiful solitary oak tree you might expect to find Rip van Winkle dozing under. The hills here are profuse with wildflowers in the springtime.

Coming very near the canyon as you hook a right, you see a well-cordoned trail leading out to a vista point, which is also the spot of an ongoing revegetation project. The "Dr. Waters" thingies that you see sticking out of the ground, resembling three-pronged gas masks, are slow-drip, nutrient-rich irrigation systems for the seedlings among them. Looking up, you get a great valley view.

Return on this spur, and follow the slanted log and cable fence down into the canyon to your right. Once in its bed, you spy an often overgrown foot trail leading off to your left, on which you can explore the wild upper reaches of Bee Canyon for over two miles.

Otherwise, turn right here on the main trail, which crosses a bridge and continues back down toward the park, with various sidetrips available down to the creek. You soon come to a grassy rest area great for picnicking, cross a bridge to your left and continue.

Just for fun, take one last little wilderness loop before re-entering the well-manicured park. As you reach the outskirts of the park, about twenty yards after the telephone pole trail siding turns into a six-by-six and stone piling fence, you see a trail leading off to your left, slightly uphill. Or skip it and head straight through the park to your car.

This small scallop of a sidetrail takes you through an interesting canyon, then up and over a densely chaparraled hillside. Wind down the trail as it hairpins right, into the park and onto the main road, where you turn left and enjoy the short shady stroll back through the green, rolling picnic grounds.

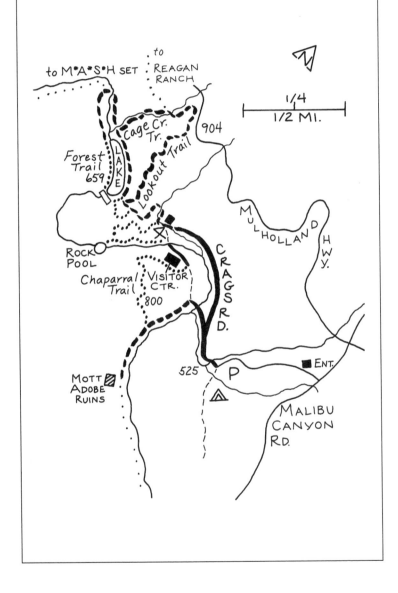

Hike 28: MALIBU CREEK STATE PARK MINI-ADVENTURE

to M*A*S*H SET

to REAGAN RANCH

Cage Cr. Tr.

Lookout Trail

904

Forest Trail 659

LAKE

1/4

1/2 MI.

MULHOLLAND HWY.

CRAGS RD.

ROCK POOL

Chaparral Trail

VISITOR CTR.

800

525

P

ENT.

MOTT ADOBE RUINS

MALIBU CANYON RD.

⚐ MALIBU CREEK STATE PARK MINI-ADVENTURE
Level 2, Hike 28

A mazelike romp through all the major attractions of Malibu Creek State Park, with tons of sidetrails, picnic areas, and exploration-friendly zones all over the place

> **DISTANCE:** 6.6-mile crazy loop, including multiple sidetrips; Elevation change: 800 feet
> **DURATION:** 2.25–4 hours
> **NOTES:** 8 A.M.–sunset; no pets permitted

DRIVING DIRECTIONS: From the 101 Freeway take the Las Virgenes Road/Malibu Canyon exit south past Mulholland Highway, and turn right at the well-signed entrance to the park. Park in the furthest possible parking area, near the cinder-block restroom building; $2 fee, trail maps available for $1.

Malibu Creek State Park is the Disneyland of parks in the Los Angeles area, with loads of fun things to do and see, including a quiet, secluded lake and a large practice boulder for rock climbers. On the board just beyond the bathrooms is a map of the park and some information about its ecosystem. Cross the main road here at the sign directing you to Backcountry Trailheads, going down the rail-tie staircase. Crossing Las Virgenes Creek, you pass a sign for Crags Road, the park's main artery, with mileage points for the sights along the way. Volunteers may be busily tending the ongoing revegetation projects that line the first part of the trail. At the wide fork, bear left, downhill—you'll be coming back on the other fork at the end of your tour.

Cross another cement bridge that has collapsed along its middle (but is still safe for foot passage) and approach a fork at a great stand of eucalypti where you turn left to take in a bit more of the creek and the ruins of the Mott Adobe. You pass a narrow utility bridge, just after which there's a sign on the right reading CHAPAR-RAL TRAIL, which you'll take to the Visitor Center on the way back from the ruins. These are nothing more than a couple of crumbling chimneys, but the creek across the way fluxes into a welcoming pool beside a beach, with oak-shaded exploration zones for several hundred yards each way.

From here, you backtrack to the Chaparral Trail, turning left at the sign. You see it's four-tenths of a mile to the visitor center. Climbing steeply up the side of a small ravine through some fragrant sage, you skirt the hill up and to your right, then cut up over a saddle. Keep right at the fork, then left as another trail goes up to the top of the hill. You immediately head down, with wonderful views of the Sugarloaf-like mountains ahead of you. A trail to your left as you descend leads to a nodular sandstone outcropping very fun to climb upon, from which you can view the Rock Pool down to your right. The Chaparral Trail takes you directly down to the visitor center, open Saturdays and Sundays only, noon to four.

Continue across the cement bridge to cross the creek, which is lined by a nearly even mixture of walnut, sycamore, elderberry, and oak. Turn left at the fork just beyond the creek for a quick jaunt to the ever-popular Rock Pool, where you are likely to be surrounded by busloads of schoolchildren on field trips weekday mornings, and hordes of relaxing families on weekends. Even though you probably won't enjoy solitude at the Rock Pool, it remains a must—its almost iconically pretty natural setting has been used as the site for a variety of outdoor movie scenes. On your right you pass the large sandstone monolith used by amateur rock climbers for practice runs. You may want to try it yourself. On the left just across from this, an amazing old sycamore beckons. Continue across the rocky wash, bearing right to the pool: a gorgeous gem with a many-tiered climbing rock at its near bank, and lots of places to sit and gaze.

As you head back on the Rock Pool trail, instead of crossing the rocky wash to go toward the rock-climbing monolith, take a side trail that angles up out of the wash to your left, curving across a hillside. You pass under shady oaks, and climb to a summit with a stone foundation of an old ranch building above it. The top of the monolith is to your left. Head straight through the wide dirt clearing, and take the path that goes straight across the clearing, down through scrub oak, curving right to head back toward the visitor center. Just before this, you turn left to go uphill again, rounding a hillock, continuing up to your left. At two wooden posts with barbed wire surrounding them you see a railroad tie with a step down into a very overgrown little trail which you're going to take down to your right. Of course, you could just backtrack on the Rock Pool trail as well. You'll learn in detail how I feel about backtracking in Hike 35, a tour of the wilder northern section of Malibu Creek State Park. Go ahead and take the Rock Pool trail back to the main road if you're not prone to sporadic adventuring, and turn left.

On your left you pass an oak-shaded picnic area. You'll be returning to this fork later to take the trail past the light green utility building you see across the way. For now, head up Crags Road as it makes a wide curve going uphill to your left, then curves right into higher country. Off to your left you spot a little sign reading NO BIKES ON TRAIL. Take the footpath it marks to visit the east shore of the lake. You immediately drop into a shady, cool, lakeside wilderness, with elderberry, walnuts, and oak lining your way, plus plenty of poison oak. This is a charming alternate trail with wooden steps down to a lakeside flat near some boulders. You can go all the way to the end of the lake and see the water running over the dam, or picnic among the rocks. Turn right past the picnic tables to continue.

The road bears left around the northeast side of the lake, where it is completely shrouded by its surrounding plant life. You meet up with the main road again and carry straight through. There's a sign reading BACKBONE TRAIL, which you'll see many times in your travels through this book. Continue through the wash; you can hear ducks quacking on the lake to your left, even though you can't see the lake. Just past a large gulley, if you look directly to your right you'll see a large old sycamore mirrored by an old oak on the other side of the gulley, and a large rock surrounded by three small rocks marking a right turn onto a trail. This is the Cage Creek Trail, which you'll take up to the upper nature trails, but first continue along the road for the best sidetrip in the park—an exploration of the lake's enchanted far bank on the charming Forest Trail. The road curves left to cross a bridge at a rush of cascades in the creek, then continues and narrows on the other side, branching off either way at a large rocky wash under a huge sycamore. Go left. If you do go right, you'll reach the M*A*S*H television show shooting site in about a mile, but the Forest Trail is far more interesting.

You head across the unmarked sandy trail through a large arid wash toward the forest you see before you. Soon you are welcomed by a dip under a large oak surrounded by a battalion of its poisonous cousins. Turn left along the cool, secluded, cricket-filled trail, always a serene respite, and not much traveled. Wend your way through tall grasses, rocky outcroppings covered in moss, fallen trees—it's one of the most beautiful parts of the park. Soon you can see the lake through the trees to your left, where sycamores and cedars mix with alders. You come right up onto the bank of the lake under a huge oak bearing the remains of a rope swing. Climb on dank, spooky steps through a crevice between two sides of a huge split rock; on the other side you can hear the water running over the dam. The trail dead-ends right at the dam. With some careful rock climbing up the side of the large sandstone hillside abutting the dam you can take any number of ready-made seats on the rocks and watch the water fall over the dam into the pool below, taking in the complicated sandstone formations pitted with pockets chiseled by the force of falling water. Please don't try walking across or climbing upon the dam.

Backtrack your way along the lake, across the wash, and over the bridge, bearing right on the trail. Bear left where you see the yellow water connector. There's a sign straight ahead marking the Cage Creek Trail. Continue straight through the tiny crossroads, going down across a gulley, under another beautiful spreading oak, through a tunnel of scrub oak, then crossing it again, heading uphill. The trail winds steeply up the hill away from the creek, across a shady oak hillside.

Soon you reach a large crossroads in the middle of a low saddle. The Yearling Trail, to your left, is a none-too-interesting one-mile loop through the grasslands to the Reagan Ranch Ranger Station. You'll be most delighted if you turn right at this crossroads onto the Lookout Trail, perhaps the best trail in the park besides the Forest Trail. This trail heads quickly uphill through some grassland. Mulholland Drive is to your left, along the telephone wires. You go over a hilltop and descend through a marshland lined with sage, then into a small scrub oak forest, at some parts quite tall, forming a chamise-laced arch. After several minutes you come to a small promontory, around which the trail curves down.

Hook around this promontory to your left, and in about a quarter of a mile you reach the main road, on which you turn left. Swing along the large curve back to the fork at the small green utility building and bear left. Then enjoy a casual stroll back across Las Virgenes Creek to your starting point.

LEVEL 3:

Daytrips

Moderately to decidedly strenuous hikes, challenging for novices, pleasantly involving for experts; half- to full-day tours of engaging areas.

RUNYON CANYON
Level 3, Hike 29

The wildest and most strenuous use of this popular citybound canyon park, plus a peaceful stroll through a posh hillside neighborhood

DISTANCE: 6.2-mile crazy loop; Elevation change: 1,000 feet
DURATION: 2.5–4 hours
NOTES: Dawn–dusk; dogs on leash permitted

DRIVING DIRECTIONS: From Franklin Avenue, take Outpost Drive north one long block to a left on Hillside Drive. Park on the street between Outpost and La Brea Avenue; no fee.

You can cut these trails up any way you please, but here you'll find a complete tour of the entire canyon: its lower reaches much beloved by dog enthusiasts and power-walkers, and its steeper trails a favorite of inner-city hikers.

To begin, follow Hillside west from La Brea to Fuller, turn right, and head through the grand stone gates to this history-laden Hollywood hideaway. Originally called No Man's Canyon, it is believed to have been a campsite of the Tongva tribe, and was bought and named by Carman Runyon, a wealthy East Coast coal merchant, as a hunting retreat in 1919. Popular Irish tenor John McCormack bought the canyon ten years later, built a villa, and added lawns, gardens, a reservoir, a pool, and tennis courts, the

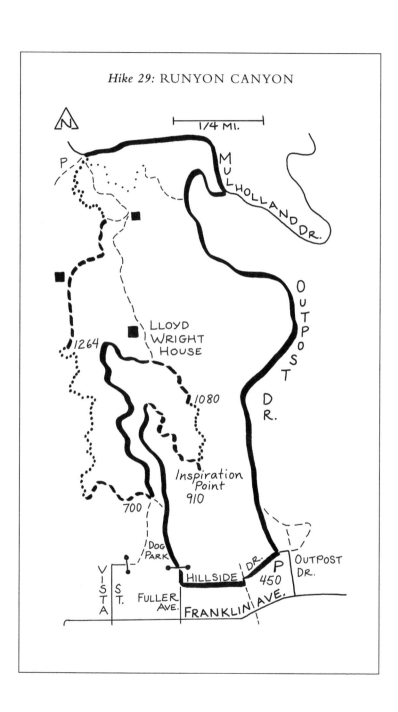

Hike 29: RUNYON CANYON

1/4 MI.

N

P

MULHOLLAND DR.

OUTPOST DR.

LLOYD WRIGHT HOUSE

1264

1080

Inspiration Point
910

700

Dog Park

VISTA ST.

FULLER AVE.

HILLSIDE DR.

P 450

OUTPOST DR.

FRANKLIN AVE.

remains of which can all be seen. In 1942, George Huntington Hartford II, heir to the A & P grocery fortune, bought the estate and renamed it The Pines. He enlisted Frank Lloyd Wright and his son, Lloyd Wright to build a country club, but neighborhood opposition quashed the project. Lloyd Wright succeeded in designing a few buildings, now in ruins, that were used by the Huntington Hartford Foundation colony for artists in the fifties. The large cottage he built still stands on private property at the top of the park, and is the subject of ongoing legal battles. Errol Flynn also lived on the property during a short period of bankruptcy in the late fifties.

To get going, pass the dog park to your left, bordered by the ruins of San Patrizio's multileveled garden, and follow the dirt road to the back of the canyon. It hairpins up to the right, passes the ruins of the tennis courts—home to a constantly entertaining array of graffiti, and occasionally still utilized by gangs of teenagers with other types of rackets. Soon you reach Inspiration Point, a wide dirt landing from which you can see clear out to Catalina on rare clear days; usually, the three battlements of business—Century City, Hollywood, and Downtown—rise from the smog below, with the cylinder of the Capitol Records building seemingly spinning in the foreground.

Just behind you is a steep graded trail with rail-tie stairs up to the eastern crest of the canyon. This is an extremely steep, but short, climb on which footing should be carefully attended. You may see tiny figures sitting on the bench at the top of hill. Below you to the right, pools appear like blue Post-it notes in the terraced backyards of ranch-style spreads and hivelike haciendas.

Get a space on the bench at the top if you can, then continue through the open plateau to the main, partially paved road through the canyon. The Lloyd Wright cottage is just up to your right. Otherwise, turn left onto the road, and wind down the center of the canyon. About two-thirds of the way down, you see an asphalt hillock/outcropping to your left along the road, directly even with Inspiration Point across the canyon. Look carefully here for a small trail leading up to your right. Take this short oleander-lined spur up to a small plateau. At the far end of the plateau is a stacked-stone pole marking a very steep path up the western ridge, through scrubby, often overgrown chaparral and a series of haunted, old lightning-scarred trees.

At the top of the first, quite steep hill, follow the trail to your right to scale a treacherous face to the highest point in the canyon. Catching your breath, you follow the trail as it heads blissfully down, around a large rocky outcropping all the way to the northern border of the canyon, where to your left you see a huge, hotel-like house that has been under construction for over a decade. Turn right just past the house, and the road will soon curve to the left under some power lines. At the fork, head down toward the reddish-brown shingled house and say hello to the horses in its attached corral as you turn left on the continuation of the main road. You can follow this road, or take any number of adventure-laden sidetrails to the northern entrance of the park, where there is a small parking lot just off Mulholland Drive.

Turn right on Mulholland, and follow it around a couple of curves to Outpost Drive, on which you turn right, twisting down steeply at first, then leveling off for a shady, peaceful stroll along the side of the street all the way back to your starting point in this high-end neighborhood that has always been a favorite of Hollywood denizens. I have been known to cut short the route from Mulholland to Outpost by turning right sharply down on the unsigned road just before Mulholland Drive at the northern entrance, then sidestepping, slipping, sliding, and even falling down the tight, chaparral-choked crevices between gated, well-manicured lawns and fortresslike tennis courts to Outpost. But I wouldn't advise it unless you're starved for some good, old-fashioned knee-scratchin'.

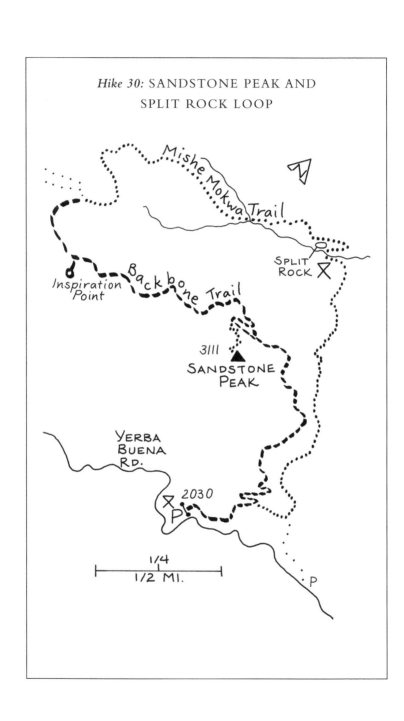

Hike 30: SANDSTONE PEAK AND
SPLIT ROCK LOOP

Mishe Mokwa Trail

Split Rock

Backbone Trail

Inspiration Point

3111
SANDSTONE PEAK

YERBA BUENA RD.

2030

1/4
1/2 MI.

P

P

✻ SANDSTONE PEAK AND SPLIT ROCK LOOP
Level 3, Hike 30

A steep trek to the highest peak in the Santa Monica Mountains, with breathtaking views, and a rambling chaparral-riparian trail along a deep, chiseled canyon

DISTANCE: 6-mile loop; Elevation change: 1,300 feet
DURATION: 2.5–4.5 hours
NOTES: Dawn–dusk; no pets permitted on Mishe Mokwa Trail

DRIVING DIRECTIONS: Take PCH north to a right on Yerba Buena Road, just past the Ventura County line. After a few miles you will see the Circle X Ranch entrance to your right. Go one mile farther and turn left into a large dirt parking lot bearing a hard-to-spot sign reading BACKBONE TRAILHEAD PARKING; no fee.

The trail to this Santa Monica Mountains begins just past the brown fence at the sign for the Backbone Trail. The wide trail rises pleasantly enough up along the road for a while, and then curves away from it, continuing to ascend steeply all the way to Sandstone Peak—a rise of over a thousand feet in a mile. You pass the Mishe Mokwa Connector Trail, your return route, after five-to-ten minutes on this climb, which takes you just high enough to see the deep purple demarcation line of the smog level below you. At the top, you skirt through a dense overgrowth of chamise and manzanita to the right of the large rocky outcropping that harbors the peak. Just before the trail dips down to the right at a large plateau, take the signed summit trail up railroad ties to your left.

It's a steep climb across loose dirt and rocks, but the views are completely worth it. Take a bag lunch in order to spend as much time up here as possible. Once you've taken in a few deep breaths of the clean, ocean-infused air, backtrack down to the main trail and follow it down the hill.

You roll along the ridge below and west of the peak toward more very interesting sandstone outcroppings. About an hour to an hour and a half into your hike, you see a small trail leading off to the left to yet another Inspiration Point, at 2,800 feet. Just ahead of you, the large sandstone mound with myriad cavelets carved into it is Exchange Peak. Go up to Inspiration Point if you like, get inspired, and return. Continuing along the main trail you pass a couple of euclayptus-ringed water towers up and to your left. From here the trail curves downhill to your right on the way to a grove of oak and sycamore popping out of the scrubby chaparral. Just beside this grove is your next crossroads, where you continue straight through onto the Mishe Mokwa Trail, reserved for hikers only. There's a little spring among the oaks and sycamores, so this crossroads can get quite wet during rainy periods. The hills around you sway with gentle wildflowers during the spring. You cross a wash, with a small grove of aspen and alder to your right, then bear left and right again around a sandstone clump toward a big sandstone cliff where, during the wet season, water rivulets and even small falls plummet from its top to the brush below.

Hook right and wander downhill through this upper country valley of sandstone wilderness, where the chaparral gets taller and taller as you go, finally rising to fifteen feet or more. In the midst of this tall scrub the trail crosses a gulley and goes back up the other side, continuing on through the scrub oak hedge, with a magnificent outcropping of sandstone formations up and to your right. You skirt the canyon to its north as the creek falls away below you. After a few minutes you descend into its shady upper banks for a moment, then right down a narrowing trail to the creek itself, under gorgeous coast live oaks and sycamores.

As you descend here the trail curves sharply right into a pleasant shade of large oaks at the site of Split Rock, a huge boulder split clear through in two places, a perfect centerpiece for a post-picnic game of hide-and-seek. From this landmark, the trail continues across the creek on a log where it leads up and out of the bed. The sign here informs you that Yerba Buena Road is only 1.7 miles ahead.

As you climb away from the creek, look over to your left to see the conical, head-with-hat-shaped sandstone formation balanced on its little pedestal at about ten o'clock. This is Balanced Rock. As you pass it to your left you see the canyon and its creek fall away far below you. You cross a feeder stream, go steeply uphill, and look to your left for another view of Balanced Rock; from this perspective it looks even more precarious. You also marvel at the sharply contoured sandstone cliffs that drop into the canyon below. This part of the trail is secluded, fragrant, and interesting for both the eyes and the feet; it's shady, too. You emerge into the sun as you head away from the canyon for an uphill climb. Just over a small saddle, take the right fork, slightly up, toward the Backbone Trail. You quickly descend to this trail where you turn left for a third of a mile of easy downhill strolling to the parking area below.

Hike 31: PORTUGUESE BEND CRAZY EIGHT

CREST RD.

CRENSHAW BLVD.

P 1180

1/4
1/2 MI.

DEL CERRO PARK

Rolling Hills

Portuguese Canyon

900

600

NARCISSA DR.

PORTUGUESE BEND

PEPPERTREE DR.

180

PALOS VERDES DR. S.

Portuguese Pt.

Inspiration Pt.

Pacific Ocean

⚶PORTUGUESE BEND CRAZY EIGHT
Level 3, Hike 31

A wild circuit of access roads and ersatz footpaths through a never-developed seaside bluff community, with awesome views of the ocean and Catalina Island

DISTANCE: 6.2-mile crazy figure eight; Elevation change: 800 feet
DURATION: 2–3.5 hours
NOTES: Dawn–dusk; dogs on leash permitted

DRIVING DIRECTIONS: From I-10, take Crenshaw Boulevard exit south all the way to its terminus at Del Cerro Park—an interesting, multicultural half-hour drive. Park along the street next to the park; no fee.

This roller-coaster of a trek on a tangle of roads and narrow footpaths through a never-finished housing development begins past the locked gate at the end of Crenshaw Boulevard, where you continue on a wide dirt road lined with anise and wild lilac. You are rewarded immediately with a spectacular view of the ocean that stays in sight throughout your hike. Turn right on the hillside trail that branches off at the first telephone pole that you come to on your right. This takes you treacherously down a steep, slippery hill past a lone, weeping pepper tree, which are prevalent in this coastal suburban wilderness. Just before the bottom of the hill you hook a sharp left uphill toward a swag of power lines. More pepper trees, and now cypress, join you. You shortly reach a T-intersection on which you turn right onto a wide dirt road, and continue downhill past a flurry of overgrown brush.

At a large fork, branch downhill to your right, continuing as the trail bends left, heading down toward the ocean. Bear left at the next fork, continuing on the main road through a huge field of twelve-foot high anise punctuated by gleaming pepper trees. Continue on the main road as it curves left just before a fenced copse of trees, and through the next crossroads where alternate roads lead up to your left and down to your right. Continue straight again when another road branches off to the right, bend left when another branches off on a sharp right, and curve to your right along the large pipe that runs along the road. You can see a profusion of wildflowers here almost all year long, with asters and morning glories taking over in the autumn. The road finally bends toward the ocean, reaching a large open space from which you can cross the street to the seaside if you wish.

To continue, take the trail to the extreme left as you enter the open space, up a small rise and soon forking off to the right, bypassing a wasteland of abandoned piping, and up into a large, unmaintained lot just beside Palos Verdes Drive. Circle to your left, until at the end of the lot you see another road leading up and to your left toward another swag of power lines. Continue past the dilapidated white house on your right; a tranquil middle-class neighborhood will appear below you through the bushes. The road curves left here, and a huge ravine opens up to your right. Continue steeply up until you reach the base of a hillock where the road branches off to the left and the right. Stay left, past a pepper tree that gracefully dips its fronds all the way to the ground, and you soon hit another fork where you head up to your right. If you turn around, you're hit by another amazing ocean view, with Catalina easily spottable even on gray days.

At the next large clearing, where the road forks down to the left or up to the right, take the foot trail leading straight up the bluff ahead of you. As you can see from this vantage point, a true maze of trails and roads laces the area. Traverse the bluff on this overgrown footpath, heading straight toward a white picket fence. A huge satellite dish beams at the sky to your right as you move into a field (mown or overgrown, depending on the season). The trail curves left, then dips down to the right after circling a bluff, wending its way down the hillside to another small fork. Take the sharp right that goes across another small plateau, then down sharply through the bottom of a ravine. Step over a pipe at the end, and turn right on the large service road.

You are now back on the main access road, which you follow all the way past the crossroads where you initially turned oceanward after trundling down the first steep hillside on your hike. Bearing right, you continue for the rest of your hike on this road as it bends lazily at first, then steeply, back up to your starting point. You could also cut out the elongated southern loop of the road by ducking into the anise-dominated wilderness on a foot trail at a small dam with an orange arrow painted on it. You wade through tall grasses on this shortcut, continuing uphill toward a large clump of pepper trees and manzanita, then left on the road at a light green water-tower, and uphill past the locked gate back to Del Cerro Park.

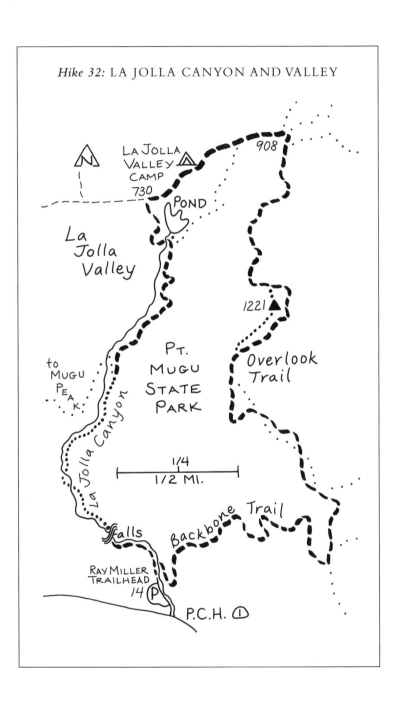

Hike 32: LA JOLLA CANYON AND VALLEY

La Jolla
Valley
Camp
730

908

Pond

La
Jolla
Valley

1221

Overlook
Trail

to
Mugu
Peak

Pt.
Mugu
State
Park

1/4
1/2 MI.

La Jolla Canyon

Backbone Trail

Falls

Ray Miller
Trailhead
14

P.C.H. ①

❧LA JOLLA CANYON AND VALLEY
Level 3, Hike 32

A steep hike up an enchanted canyon with a pleasant waterfall to a quiet grassland with a placid pond, then a fortifying walk with views back to the ocean at Point Mugu

DISTANCE: 8-mile loop; Elevation change: 900 feet
DURATION: 2.75–5 hours
NOTES: Dawn–dusk; no pets permitted

DRIVING DIRECTIONS: Take PCH all the way past Malibu north to Point Mugu, just across the Ventura County line. Thornhille Broome Beach and Campground will appear coastside, and to your right, a sign directing you into La Jolla Canyon. Park in the very large, paved Ray Miller Trailhead parking lot; restrooms are available; no fee.

Overcast and cool even on a sunny Los Angeles day, La Jolla Canyon is most impressive in mid-spring, when giant coreiopsis, looking like black-eyed Susans gone wild and monstrous, choke the middle reaches of the canyon, and the valley above is dusted with delicate wildflowers. Begin by swinging past the yellow gate at the end of the lot, follow the main road for a bit, and soon you're on the La Jolla Canyon Trail, dry and sandy at first, and greener as you go along. Half a mile into your hike you rise on a set of steps carved into the stone of La Jolla Canyon Falls. The falls are just a trickle during the summer, but always pleasant, looking formal and ancient, like a lost set from some silent movie involving moonlit ceremonies led by high priestesses. Crossing the stream here, pick up the trail on the other side of the falls and hike up another small carved-stone staircase, climbing beside the furtive rush of the creek below no matter what the season.

After several minutes of climbing you come to a fork in the road. The small spur to the left leads down into the canyon and through the mountains to your northwest into the La Jolla Valley, where you can "bag" Mugu Peak if you like. We're going to keep heading up the trail, entering the loveliest and shadiest part of the journey. As you continue climbing, the valley stretches to your left, its almost imperceptible rolling hills covered in tall grasses and laced with coyote trails. Bear left at the next fork, down into the canyon, and soon you reach a pond nearly hidden by tule and reeds. Go straight around the perimeter. Wildlife viewing here is always possible provided you remain still and quiet: rabbit, fox, and quail dash around the shoreline or chase each other through the tangles of coastal scrub that encroach upon lusher waterside foliage.

Past the pond, trails lead just about everywhere: some straight across the valley and others to the thickets and groves that dot it like lost islands. At the top of the grassland is the La Jolla Valley Camp, a favorite of Southern California backpackers, and a nice, high, secluded spot for picnickers, meditators, and afternoon nappers. Turn right on a wide dirt road, climbing steadily uphill. You pass a small trail leading up from around the other side of the pond, and soon after that hit a large crossroads, where you could extend this loop by turning left on the deserted Guadalasco Trail into Wood Canyon. For now, turn right, toward the ocean, onto the signed Overlook Trail.

Continue along the ridge toward the ocean with the spiky blue and purple apices of Boney Mountain undulating to your left.

As you near the sea, the mountains melt into vast ocean vistas for some of the best views on the coast. Swinging left, you soon come to a well-marked turnoff for the Backbone Trail. Turn right, and either dawdle or quickstep down its twists and turns through coastal scrub to your starting point.

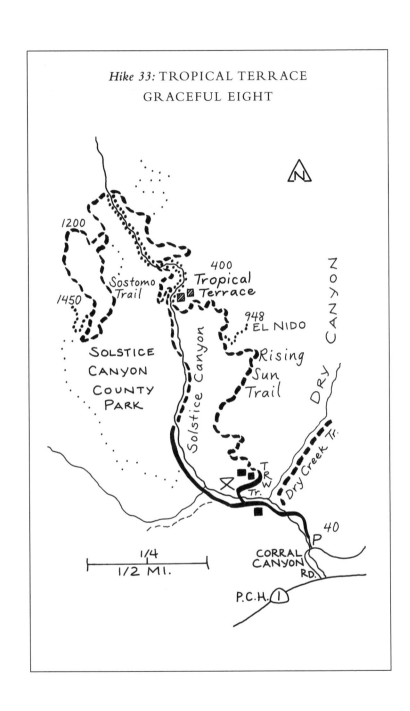

Hike 33: TROPICAL TERRACE
GRACEFUL EIGHT

N

1200

Sostomo
Trail

1450

400
Tropical
Terrace

948
EL NIDO

Rising
Sun
Trail

SOLSTICE
CANYON
COUNTY
PARK

Solstice Canyon

DRY CANYON

TRW
Tr.

Dry Creek Tr.

1/4
1/2 MI.

CORRAL
CANYON
RD.

40
P

P.C.H. 1

ꙮ TROPICAL TERRACE
GRACEFUL EIGHT
Level 3, Hike 33

The grand tour of Solstice Canyon Park, including funky ruins, waterfalls and cascades, trailblazing, rock-climbing, and a great blur of wildflowers in spring

DISTANCE: 7-mile figure eight; Elevation change: 1,800 feet

DURATION: 3–5 hours

NOTES: 8 A.M.–5 P.M.; no pets permitted

DRIVING DIRECTIONS: Take PCH north past Malibu Canyon Road and Pepperdine University to turn right on Corral Canyon Road—look for the Union 76 gas station on the right. In a few hundred yards, just after the road curves right, turn left into the gated entrance to Solstice Canyon Park. There's a small dirt lot immediately to your right, and a larger one just up the road to your left near the visitors' center; no fee.

The main, partially paved trail that leads off beyond the visitor center into the canyon goes easily and directly to Tropical Terrace, a fifties ranch-style estate built by popular African-American architect Paul R. Williams and destroyed by fire in 1982. Its ruins and attendant pools and cascades are a wonderful place for exploring, picnicking, or just hanging out. The easy walk up the canyon and back is great for kids, if a bit overrun on weekends. Here we'll be reaching Tropical Terrace by climbing high up into the overgrown hills to your right on the Rising Sun Trail, then clambering up the creek at the Terrace to join a rarely traversed loop through a scrub oak forest on the Sostomo Trail. Just past the visitor center, turn right on the paved TRW Trail, beginning steeply uphill.

As the trail curves up and to the left, a postmodern cliffside estate, built around the time the Roberts designed home at Tropical Terrace burned down, juts out over a precipice, looking like a crashed spaceship. Just as the silolike TRW building begins to come into sight at the top of the hill, look for a small sign to your left, directing you toward the Rising Sun Trail, .15 miles ahead. Veer left here, and at the fork soon after take a sharp right. Go back up toward the TRW building, across the parking lot toward the private residence at number 3455, where you make another sharp right on the Rising Sun trailhead.

From here, it's a brisk climb across the overgrown hillsides to the south of the canyon, rife with leggy scrub and vines, and dusted with an array of unusual wildflowers in the spring, to a steep drop down to Tropical Terrace. At the top of the Rising Sun Trail, a signpost announces the El Nido Trail, a short sidetrip up to the top of the hill to your right where there is a cozy nest, just large enough for one person, or possibly two, to hide away in. Circumnavigate the canyon below, then head sharply downhill, where the babble of the many cascades that fall past Tropical Terrace comes into earshot.

The ruins themselves have a slight stink to them, especially in the summer, but you can hardly help exploring them. To the right of the ruins, a welcoming grotto of small waterfalls and pools beckons from among palm trees in a tiny, junglelike setting that can be packed with sightseers even on weekdays. The Sostomo Trail begins here to the left of Tropical Terrace, and rises steeply again up the hillside to the south. If you yearn for a little solitude at this point, you'll find it farther up the creek. Continue past the sometimes crowded cascade area, and at first simply scout for a private place to sit and enjoy the sound of the creek. You'll find that the steep, rocky bed remains navigable with a bit of low-level rock-climbing. A few places where boulders have created seemingly impassable walls can be tricky, but there is always a way around these obstructions if you look closely and take your time. Follow the stream uphill, completely alone now, with cascades and inviting pools all the way, to a place about half a mile upstream where the Sostomo Trail crosses the bed. Some of the clearest and deepest swimming holes on the coast can be found here, especially enticing on a hot summer day.

The Sostomo Trail crosses the creek at a flat spot with a large, shallow pool just beyond it. Turn left here, and head uphill. A dozen yards after leaving the creek, you see another abandoned structure to your left, this one older than Tropical Terrace and now merely a stone shell. It is far more foresty and cooler here than it is on the Rising Sun Trail, with a variety of ferns curling and breathing in the damp riparian air. You head steeply uphill, hairpinning back toward the ocean, and soon come upon a sign reading DEER VALLEY LOOP. Keep left, heading slightly downhill now, and then right at the next fork, which leads you to a wider trail that takes you all the way to 1,200 feet. There, a scramble up a short spur to the top of Solstice Peak affords unparalleled ocean views. Back on the trail, make a U-turn downhill, joining the Deer Valley Loop for a bit, and shortly merging with the Sostomo Trail to the point at which you emerged from your climb up the creek.

Head straight across the bed on the Sostomo Trail as it rises high on the hill above the canyon, then descends back to Tropical Terrace. At this point, you join the cyclists and lookie-loos and picnicking families for a pleasant creekside walk on wide, partially paved Solstice Canyon Road, passing a few bucolic private residences on your way back down to the parking area.

⚘BRONSON CANYON AND
HOLLYWOODLAND LOOP
Level 3, Hike 34

*A steady climb to Mt. Hollywood, west to pass under the Hollywood
sign, and a steep curl down through the original Hollywood Hills neighborhood*

> **DISTANCE:** 8.8-mile loop, with alternate sidetrip to the
> "Bat Cave"; Elevation change: 1,340 feet
> **DURATION:** 3–5 hours
> **NOTES:** 6 A.M.–10 P.M.; dogs on leash permitted

DRIVING DIRECTIONS: Park on the street around Cheremoya
Avenue and Franklin Avenue, between Beachwood and Bronson
just east of the 101 Freeway; no fee.

This hearty hike up the western side of Griffith Park is popular
with local dog-walkers and exercise fanatics, and includes a tour
through "Hollywoodland," the first housing development to colo-
nize the Hollywood Hills in the 1920s. The development also gave
us the famed Hollywood sign (the "land" rotted away years ago).
Begin by walking up Cheremoya Avenue to turn right on Chula
Vista Street, then left on Bronson Avenue, which curves right on a
steady uphill grade to meet the entrance to the park. Just inside the
gates is a rolling playground and picnicking hillside, beyond which
you see a fire road curving up to your right. Take this short, easy
spur to a long-abandoned quarry known as the Bronson Caves,
whose main "cave" is actually just an access tunnel through a huge,

Hike 34: BRONSON CANYON AND
HOLLYWOODLAND LOOP

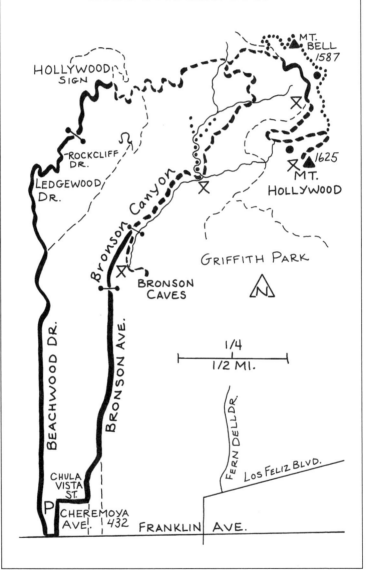

MT. BELL 1587

HOLLYWOOD SIGN

ROCKCLIFF DR.

LEDGEWOOD DR.

1625

MT. HOLLYWOOD

Bronson Canyon

GRIFFITH PARK

N

BRONSON CAVES

1/4
1/2 MI.

BEACHWOOD DR.

BRONSON AVE.

FERN DELL DR.

LOS FELIZ BLVD.

CHULA VISTA ST.

P
CHEREMOYA AVE. | 432   FRANKLIN AVE.

unmined rock in the center of the quarry. This cool cubbyhole has been used, and continues to be a favorite filming site, for everything from Westerns to cheesy alien flicks, and served as the outdoor shot of the "Bat Cave" for the *Batman* television series in the 1960s. Steep, makeshift trails to the south and east up to the rim of the old quarry allow fun scrambling to views of the entire Los Angeles basin on clear days.

Back on the main road, turn right to pass through a small gate and enter Bronson Canyon. To your right after a hundred yards or so is an old cement drainage system decorated by graffiti and often crowded by gangs of young skate punks perfecting their X Games moves. The trail bends to the right, where a small grassy area makes a perfect hidden spot for family get-togethers or hippie-style outdoor commitment ceremonies. Across the trail from this area, a network of tiny footpaths laces the canyon bottom. It's often completely overgrown, but a great place for young adventurers.

Heading left over a spring, the main trail rises steeply and steadily as the canyon falls away below you. As you turn right at the last bend, stop at the clearing, look back, and see all of Hollywood at your feet. Just after this bend, the trail branches both left and right—turn right for a brief, entertaining loop over the two highest peaks in Griffith Park. Follow the trail up, most likely fighting off the dust of passing equestrians from the nearby Sunset Ranch stables, turn left on the main road, and follow it uphill as it curves to the right at a saddle. The road here dips down into the San Fernando Valley. Mt. Bell, just to your right, can be reached on a smaller footpath at the crossroads. This path takes you around the back of Mt. Bell to its north side, from which you can see the steep wilds of Griffith Park abruptly adjoining the flat grids of Burbank and Glendale. Continue around the backside of the mountain, and pick up a still smaller trail, barely wide enough for one person, to your right at a sign reading VENT. You can cut across the ridge directly south toward Mt. Hollywood. Below you to your left are the greens of the Griffith Park golf course, with the eastern valley disappearing into the smog among the foothills. The bald pate of Mt. Hollywood, with its battalion of seldom-used picnic tables and stray solar panels, is inhospitable and often windy even on still days, so you are likely to have it all to yourself.

Once you've taken in the views from atop Mt. Hollywood, head back across its wide, bare apex and make the first left as you descend, connecting to a winding firebreak road that switches back and forth to the paved road (now closed to vehicles) that you see below you. You meet up with this road, turning right at a deserted grassy knoll. Follow the road back up the hill, and turn left onto the dirt road beyond the white locked gate. Continue along the northern edge of the canyon, passing a wooden marker signifying the trail on which you initially climbed up, continuing to your right at crossings. Ten to twenty minutes on this trail brings you to a fork where a sharp curve to the left leads down to Sunset Ranch, where you can rent horses. Bear right, where, five minutes farther along, the dirt trail abuts a paved road just beneath the Hollywood sign. This is your best view of the sign, (which looks better in photographs and on film than in person). If you turn right on the paved road and bear left at the next fork you can follow a trail up the hill behind the sign. Otherwise, turn left on the paved road. You soon see a blue pool, a pergola, a terrace, a modishly curved 1960s roof, and finally a small white gate. Pass through it into Hollywoodland.

Turn left beyond the gate. The remainder of the hike takes you steeply downhill through that particular mix of stern modern architectural exercises and faux Gothic fantasias that has always been possible only in Hollywood. Turn right at Rockcliff Drive, curve down to your right, and make a hairpin left on Ledgewood Drive, which will take you to Beachwood Canyon Drive. At 3106 Ledgewood you pass Oz, a fanciful private garden that glitters all the way up a fenced-in hillside. Turn right on Beachwood Canyon Drive, and stroll through the neighborhood, past Beachwood Canyon Village, featuring a decent coffee shop and one of the most entertaining community bulletin boards around, all the way down to the traffic light at Franklin Avenue. Cheremoya Avenue is just one block to your left.

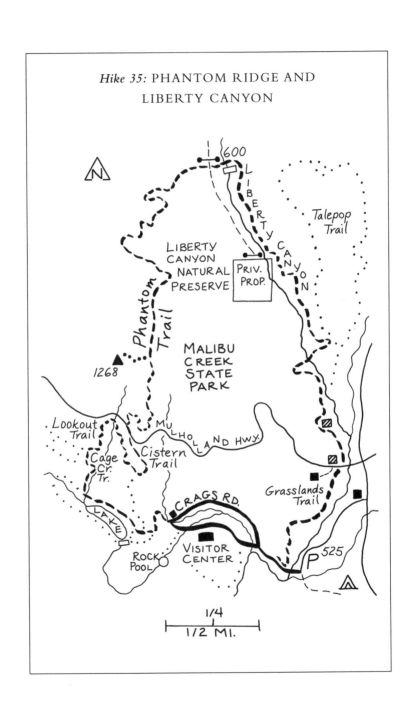

Hike 35: PHANTOM RIDGE AND
LIBERTY CANYON

600

N

LIBERTY CANYON

Talepop Trail

LIBERTY
CANYON
NATURAL
PRESERVE

PRIV.
PROP.

Phantom Trail

1268

MALIBU
CREEK
STATE
PARK

Lookout Trail

MULHOLLAND HWY.

Cage
Cr.
Tr.

Cistern
Trail

Grasslands
Trail

LAKE

CRAGS RD.

Rock
Pool

VISITOR
CENTER

P 525

1/4
1/2 MI.

✿PHANTOM RIDGE AND LIBERTY CANYON
Level 3, Hike 35

A brief tour of Malibu Creek State Park, a tough climb to an eerie ridge, and a peaceful descent through riparian and grassland wildernesses

DISTANCE: 8.6-mile loop; Elevation change: 800 feet
DURATION: 2.75–5 hours
NOTES: 8 A.M.–sunset; no pets permitted

DRIVING DIRECTIONS: From the 101 Freeway take the Las Virgenes Road/Malibu Canyon exit south past Mulholland Highway, and turn right at the well-marked entrance to the park. Park in the farthest possible parking area, near the cinderblock restrooms; $2 fee, trail maps available for $1.

For a full tour of Malibu Creek State Park, refer to Hike 28, which will give you more than enough information for a whole day's worth of exploration around the park's many enticing attractions. Here the mission is to explore the wilder, stranger, less apparently attractive, northern half of the park, up on the wild and lonely Phantom Ridge Trail for the best inland views of any hike in this book, and down along a friendly country road through Liberty Canyon, skirting private property all the way.

You begin, as in Hike 28, at the far end of the parking lot, crossing the paved road toward the Backcountry Trailheads onto Crags Road, the main artery through the southern half of the park. If you have all day, explore the park as described in Hike 28 before venturing north. The quickest way to the Phantom Ridge Trail is to take Crags Road directly west to the Cage Creek Trail, signified by a yellow water connector to your right at a junction just north of the lake. This winding trail around canyon fingers under scrub oak canopies will take you quickly to a large cross-roads, where you turn right on the Lookout Trail. The Lookout Trail loops around toward Mulholland, then back, and reaches a small promontory where the trail heads downhill to the left toward Crags Road. Stop here and look directly behind you to your left. You see a ruthlessly steep hillside of railroad ties. Climb it quickly, just to get it over with.

You are now on the Cistern Trail, a footpath that wends its way on a low ridge to its namesake, a shallow cement runoff collector just south of Mulholland on a small sage-ringed platform. The trail drops you unceremoniously out into a parking turnoff on the south side of Mulholland. Turn left on the highway, straight ahead as the trail ends. Continue for sixty to seventy yards, crossing where you see the Horse Crossing sign. The brown sign on the opposite side of the street here shows you where your trail starts. Pass between two partially burned poles onto the Phantom Ridge Trail, which immediately begins switchbacking up the hill, steeper as it goes. You soon find yourself high up on the ridge, still climb-ing, with views all around of the sheer, graceful mountains of the park and the rocky crags toward Topanga.

Continue onward and upward. It's unrelentingly steep for a good while, but the views are sublime. Occasionally, the trail joins the ridgetop fire road, then dips down into the forest again. Far below you can see the bedroom communities of the Agoura Hills with their modified cookie-cutter houses, and closer in, the Liberty

Canyon Trail, which you'll be taking on your return. Las Virgenes Road, a 101 Freeway feeder road, moves busily but noiselessly far, far below you to your right. Make sure to take all the signed cut-offs instead of going over the hills at the top of the ridge on the fire road. These harbor lovely archways of manzanita, scrub oak, and elderberry. Sage is your most constant companion on this part of the trip. It huddles in clumps along the trail, whispering and shivering in the wind and sharing its sharp, smoky scent.

After crossing the highest point on the ridge you rejoin the fire road once more and follow the little brown arrow, bending right on the fire road then almost immediately left. Here you swing around the righthand wall of a small, elderberry-filled ravine. Yucca whipplei join the sage in the undergrowth on the hill to the right. Going downhill, the trail loops around to head northeast toward Liberty Canyon. Another brown arrow tells you to turn right over a saddle. Go straight through across the fire road at the next arrow, and shortly after begin winding earnestly downhill. Enjoy the shade and quiet here on the lower part of this trail, filled with a hundred greens in spring and softened by red and orange leaves in the autumn.

Soon you are walking along the right hillside bank of a very steep and narrow ravine down to your left, filled with water during the wet season. A few more lazy curves down and you are in the grasslands, passing strange metal wreckage, crossing a little gulley, and heading out toward a grove of huge eucalyptus trees, while coyotes yap in the hills to your left. You cut directly between the eucalypti over a large log and come to a private road. Straight across it you can see some foot trails beaten into the grasslands. Join the most well-trod one, slightly to your right and across the street.

The first time I did this hike, I came the other way, up Liberty Canyon, and couldn't find the Phantom Ridge Trail connector. I ended up scaling a hill between two private properties to the south of this crossing, getting lost and entangled in a seemingly endless ten-foot-high tangle of thick chaparral, and climbing up to walk across the tops of manzanita trees to find a coyote trail leading to a fire road, all because I feel unwaveringly averse to backtracking. It was exciting, but it was also life-threatening, which brings me to probably the best lesson to keep in mind as you start doing some of the more difficult hikes in the book: If you get lost, do not be too proud to backtrack unless you are actively looking for some sort of risky, cathartic, near-death experience and a whole lot of bruises, nicks, and cuts. Of course, when I later found that the Phantom Ridge Trail connector continued literally right across the road, I felt like a darned fool.

Anyway, cross the private road and take the footpath through a large patch of gourd vines right along the chain-link fence of a private property, turning left at the corner of the fence where two large rocks act as sentinels. Soon you see a cement dam lined with chain link to your right. Turn right toward it and pass along the fence, then right again on the trail that you find directly past it. Now you are in Liberty Canyon, and you'll be taking this trail with just a few minor directions all the way back to your car.

You see the State Park Boundary sign soon after, pass through grassland, then amble pleasantly creekside, with the dense banks below you to your right, and back and forth on the verge between these two environments. Unfortunately, you follow telephone wires, but they don't noisily buzz as so many do. This is a pleasant, meditative walk. You circle up to circumvent private property, and back down again after a long stretch through the grasslands beside the creek. The sign for the Talepop Trail appears to the left, but who wants to go uphill again? Stay on the Liberty Canyon Trail, which soon dips under shady oaks and passes by perhaps the largest gourd vine expanse in the area. The gourd vines look like sweet little sci-fi creatures or the eggs of some exotic bird (or like alien body-snatching pods, if you're in a darker mood). Soon after that you rise shortly up, then back downhill, bearing left. A brown post up ahead of you signals where you'll make a sharp, hairpin right.

A signpost announces that you are now on the Grasslands Trail. Heading right down into the creek, you cross it on a cunning wood-and-steel bridge erected in January of 1994 by Matt Spigel's Eagle Project, Boy Scout Troop 126, Woodland Hills, California—great job, Eagle Scouts! You rise up out of the creek to follow a barbed-wire fence on your right, and curve left with the trail at the T-intersection. The trail edges around a small power station on its way to Mulholland Highway. The grasslands here are covered with wildflowers in the spring, and are beautiful even in the late summer with their surprising varieties of dry brown, yellow, auburn, and mulberry. You pass by the site of the Sepulveda Adobe on your right, where some sort of construction has been taking place for a very long time next to the crumbling stove and chimney corner that is the only sign of the historic site.

You then pass through an opening in a wire fence onto Mulholland Highway. Go straight across, jogging slightly left, almost to the mailbox reading 26986. Here you turn left down onto the Grasslands Trail, where there's another opening in a wooden post fence. Crags Road is just under a mile ahead of you; a very easy walk through tall, singing grasses. Turn left on Crags Road at the yellow water connector. If you feel like it, it's fun to give yourself a final rush by skidding and slipping down a nearly vertical hillside path as others have obviously done to cut off the last lazy curve in the trail. It's just a skip, hop, and a jump from here across the creek and up to the parking lot.

⚘BIG SYCAMORE AND
SERRANO CANYONS
Level 3, Hike 36

An engaging hike through a capacious Point Mugu-area canyon woodland, up and across a murmuring grassland, and down spirit-laden, overgrown Serrano Canyon

DISTANCE: 10-mile loop; Elevation change: 1,200 feet
DURATION: 3–5.5 hours

DRIVING DIRECTIONS: Take PCH all the way north to the Point Mugu area. Turn right, with the Thornhille Broome State Beach to your left, at the turnoff for the Sycamore Canyon Campground Parking Area. Go right past the entrance booth, and turn left immediately to find at least an acre of day-use parking; $3 fee when manned.

From the parking lot, walk all the way back through the campground to a gate where there's a sign for the Big Sycamore Canyon Trail to begin this sometimes soothing, sometimes eerie, magical hike through two very different canyons in Point Mugu State Park. This is one of my favorite hikes. Even if you are partial to the Angeles Forest, or really only interested in bagging peaks, head out past the Ventura County line one day to mine this gem for yourself.

Slip past the yellow gate, and you're off.

You see a little SCENIC TRAIL sign to your left, which makes a nice, short sidetrip. Our path goes all the way up through the center of Big Sycamore Canyon on a casual ascent for about four

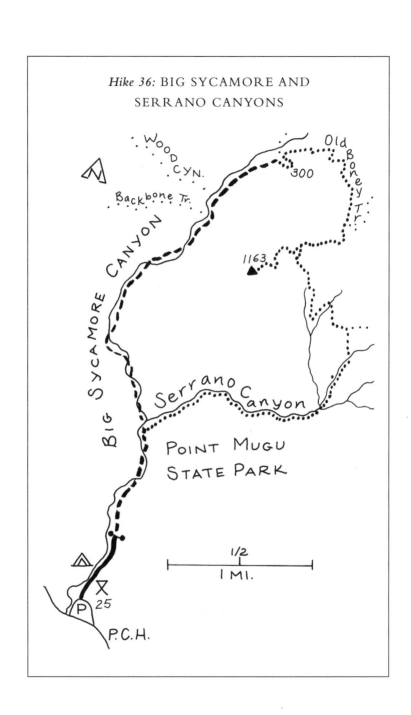

Hike 36: BIG SYCAMORE AND
SERRANO CANYONS

Wood Cyn.

Old Boney Tr.

300

Backbone Tr.

1163

BIG SYCAMORE CANYON

Serrano Canyon

POINT MUGU
STATE PARK

1/2
1 MI.

25

P

P.C.H.

miles, until we reach the Backbone/Old Boney Trail that will take us up to tranquil Sycamore Valley, and down through haunted Serrano Canyon to reconnect with the Big Sycamore Trail about a mile up from the starting point.

You'll see at once how the canyon got its name: These are some of the biggest sycamore trees you're likely to run across. There are many opportunities to go down to the creek, which is dry except in the wet season.

Keep on the main trail when you see the Overlook Trail heading off to the left fifteen to twenty-five minutes into your hike. About twenty to thirty-five minutes after that you see water pump number 29, and slightly before that the trail leading off to your right into Serrano Canyon. This is your return route. Continue on the main trail, crossing the creek several times, very wetly and muddily during the wet season, and with leftover pools during the dry months at certain crossings. After a while the sycamores start to share their space with oaks of equal grandeur; a particularly impressive grove houses a picnic area on your left.

About fifty to eighty minutes into your hike you see a sign to your left reading BACKBONE TRAIL TO OVERLOOK TRAIL. Don't take this; it simply means you're less than a mile from a righthand turnoff going up to the valley and then down to Serrano Canyon.

Not long after you come to a large fork in the road; keep to your right. Morning glories line your path, and wildflowers abound here in the spring. Even more beautiful are the thousands of shades of green that fight for the spotlight on the hills after rains.

As you near your turn off, the upper canyon widens into rolling meadows. You see water pump number 17 on your left, and to your right, a sign for the Old Boney Trail. Turn here to begin the steepest part of your hike, continuing on foot-traffic-only paths all the way through Serrano Canyon until you meet up again with the Big Sycamore Trail.

Start by passing through an overgrown canyon finger, then cross the creek for a left hairpin uphill to begin your ascent to a little over 1,000 feet in the next mile. The trail leads you back out for an overlook of the canyon you've just come through, then curves away from it on a long, slow, steady uphill curve. Off to your left you see Old Boney, blue and rough with crags. At the top of the first hill you continue past the Backbone Trail sign up to the apex, from which you get a spectacular 360-degree view. The trail hooks right and goes along the top of the ridge, quickly down into an overgrown hedge of chaparral, then leads to a barbed-wire fence where it hooks right to continue through the scrub oak and chamise maze. At the end of it there's a fork to the right going up to the peak above you at 1,163 feet. Take this quick sidetrip or keep to your left along the edge of the mountain. You descend into an even more overgrown processional chaparral arch with slightly leggier hedges along either side of you, then curve left into the valley below, across a whispering grassland.

You curve landward into a small canyon arm and cross it, curving back up the other side through another chaparral archway. Heading across more grassland, look hard to find the wooden post with the faded arrow instructing you to bear right. If you can't spot it, just start to head downhill on this second stretch of grassland, perhaps startling a fox from its hunt, and come to a place where a trail forks off to the right, with the one you're on leading straight ahead. Make a right turn here. The trail leading straight ahead will take you to Serrano Road, then Deer Creek Road, dropping you out on PCH several miles south of Big Sycamore Canyon.

Turn right and head down Serrano Valley toward Serrano

Canyon. More rolling grassland awaits you here. There's a strange little metal shed sheltering some sort of antiquated and dilapidated mechanical contraption to your left about halfway down. Continue down to your right into the canyon just after passing a twisted deadwood sculpture where another fork leads back up into the grassland. Shade awaits, as does a huge overgrowth of poison oak. Turn left and follow the trail. You soon head down into dense reeds, poison oak, scrub oak, and chamise, going down a railroad-tie stairwell to the bottom of a creek, then across and back up on more ties. It's very secluded down here among the crickets and the cattails. Heading down into Serrano Canyon, you wind through a dense riparian wilderness rife with a larger variety of plants than are usually found on hikes in this book. The trail can be ragged at times and lined with stinging nettle, so wear long pants.

The creek in Serrano Canyon runs even during the dry season. It's much shadier and more sylvan here than Big Sycamore Canyon, with lither sycamores lining the path, sharing space with scrub oak and other types of riparian flora. Sometimes the trail leads straight down and through the creekbed, so be prepared to get wet during or after rains.

This is an enchanted canyon: shady, lush, and cozy, with a slight air of menace. You cross the stream several times. Take your time here—don't rush through this captivating place. The wind picks up. You listen to the rich soprano rumble of the sycamore leaves. All too soon you rise up on a set of graded stone steps on your way to rejoin Big Sycamore Canyon. But wait! Another set of steps leads you back down. The smell of anise surrounds you. Large boulders fallen from the hillside to your right litter the trail. Again, the sycamores greet you with their waterfall impersonations. A huge, multipronged streamside oak invites you to slip among its joints and hollows. The trees become larger, the sycamore leaves like dinosaur footprints. Birds and crickets call back and forth. Scrub takes over as a gateway to even larger sycamores. Soon you turn left onto the Big Sycamore Canyon Trail, and head back through its calmer, wider vista to the yellow gate, past the campground to your car.

ꙮ EAGLE ROCK EIGHT
Level 3, Hike 37

A brisk climb to Eagle Rock, Topanga's premier landmark, a gentle stroll along Temescal Ridge, and back on the rugged Garapito Canyon and Musch Trails

DISTANCE: 10.6-mile figure eight; Elevation change: 1,600 feet

DURATION: 3.5–6 hours

NOTES: Dawn–dusk; no pets permitted

DRIVING DIRECTIONS: From the 101 Freeway, take Topanga Canyon Boulevard exit south, pass Ventura Boulevard, and twist several miles steeply up into the hills, nearly to the village of Topanga. Turn left on Entrada Road at the sign for Topanga Canyon State Park, follow it up for about a mile, and bear left where it turns into Colina Road, remaining on Entrada Road to its terminus at Trippet Ranch. Turn right past the first ranch buildings, then left into the very large main parking lot; no fee.

This varied hike through the golden west begins on the wide dirt road that leads through the split-wood fence at the far end of the Trippet Ranch parking lot, taking you immediately to a fork. To the left is a nature center; continue to your right and turn left at the large signed fork—Eagle Rock is 1.8 miles ahead on this well-graded pathway.

Soon you come to a wide vista where the Santa Ynez trail leads off to your right. Notice the NO ALCOHOLIC BEVERAGES sign. The

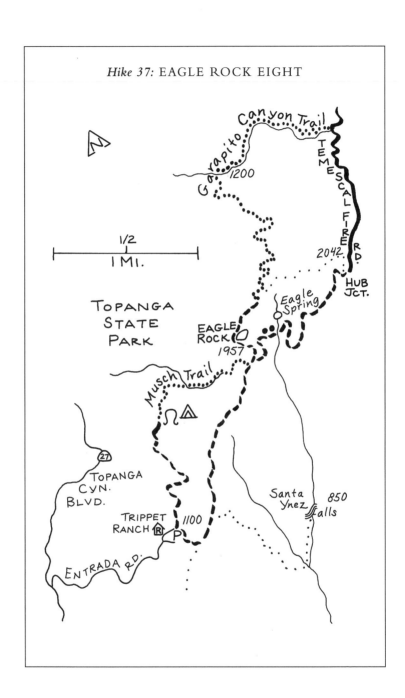

Hike 37: EAGLE ROCK EIGHT

Garapito Canyon Trail

TEMESCAL FIRE RD.

1200

2042

HUB JCT.

1/2

1 MI.

TOPANGA
STATE
PARK

Eagle
Spring

EAGLE
ROCK

1957

Musch Trail

27

TOPANGA
CYN.
BLVD.

Santa
Ynez Falls   850

TRIPPET
RANCH ℝ P 1100

ENTRADA RD.

Santa Ynez Waterfall is, unfortunately, a haven for teenage and young adult partiers, and is littered with trash and smattered with graffiti. Explore it on your own if you wish and continue along the main trail. You rise above the rolling meadows and oak woodland below you, with the mountains directly west of you snugly harboring their hilltop haciendas.

As you near Eagle Rock, you hit a large crossroads where four trails branch off. The center trail goes straight up to Eagle Rock. You can cut the trip short here if you like by experiencing Eagle Rock, which is the large sandstone formation you see on your way up, and then hiking back down and taking the Musch Trail back to Trippet Ranch, which leads off to your left here. To carry on with our long figure eight, stay on the main trail to your far right; the Eagle Springs Fire Road to Hub Junction. As you swing around your first curve Eagle Rock pops out at you, impressive and vaguely shaped like an eagle's head. Actually, it doesn't look like any sort of representation of an eagle except by the most outlandish leaps of the imagination.

Pass by Eagle Springs, which has a tiny foot trail into it, on your left. There is nothing much to see here, but it's a lovely shaded creek, in the wet season quite full of water, though riddled with poison oak. Past this turnoff you begin a sharp ascent to your right. Look back at Eagle Rock here. Can you see the eagle yet? Check out the hole the wind has blown in the top middle peak just before the highest point, which, when you get close to it, produces an eerie low whistle.

After another 1.3 miles of fairly brisk uphill climbing you reach the signboard and blue outhouse of the Hub Junction. Turn left here onto the Temescal Ridge Fire Road, as signed. Again, you could cut your hike short at this point by making a sharp left onto the Eagle Rock Fire Road, which leads back along the other side of the rock, and from there taking the Musch Trail back down to Trippet Ranch.

The Temescal Ridge Trail is a nearly flat, very winding, meditative walk. After what seems almost no time at all you come to another crossroads. To the right is the Bent Arrow trail to Mulholland Drive, only three-tenths of a mile more—you can go up the trail and collect more views of the valley. On your left is the Garapito Canyon Trail, a foot-traffic-only trail that's blissful if you've run into a healthy string of mountain bikers all the way up. Turn left down the small footpath. You soon wind down into the shade of the canyon, with its tall, arching manzanita and toyon trees. This is about as wild as you can get while still benefiting from a trail. There are lots of places to explore in the creek, and during the wet season, you also may be finding yourself fording your way right across small waterfalls.

On your way down, you cross the stream many times. At a particularly wide crossing, at a triple-trunked oak just ahead of you, the trail turns abruptly to the left beyond the creek. Here you begin your long, winding ascent from the canyon to where it junctions with the Eagle Rock Fire Road just above the rock itself.

After thirty to fifty minutes of twisty climbing requiring some light bushwhacking Eagle Rock appears ahead of you. Five to ten minutes later you reach the fire road, on which you turn right, toward the rock.

For a treat, take one of the sidetrails up to the left as you reach the apex of the fire road, to the top of the rock, which you can climb along at your own risk. Back on the fire road, head downhill to the junction, and make a sharp right onto the narrow Musch Trail. You wind down into a peaceful canyon, this one absolutely riddled with poison oak, but shady and cool and more spacious than the rugged recesses of Garapito Canyon.

Head out into a patch of grassland, then through oak and eucalyptus forests, again in the shade, for the final leg of your hike. Soon you come to a split-wood fence demarcating a small stand of horse corrals and picnic tables. Cross the asphalt road at the trail sign, bearing left, and turn right on the larger dirt road when the smaller foot trail ends. You can turn left again at the trail sign a short way beyond this, or simply do this whole small section on the road you crossed.

Wind along chaparral hillsides: There's nothing new to see, but it's a lovely stroll. Last time I was finishing up a long hike on this pleasant path that leads back to the parking lot through a variety of riparian, woodland and grassland zones, a tiny tyke stumbling along with a small family group beamed up at me and announced excitedly, "We're going for a walk!" The lower trails here, and the nature trail around Trippet Ranch, are great for small kids.

Near the end of your hike you cross a footbridge over the creek, and head into some more grassland where you see a metal corral and a split fence. Cross it to arrive at a paved road, on which you turn left. The buildings of Trippet Ranch are visible above the trees straight ahead of you. Just a short walk is left on this paved trail to a kiosk bearing event schedules and information about the ingenious Chumash Indian uses of the local flora at the edge of the parking lot.

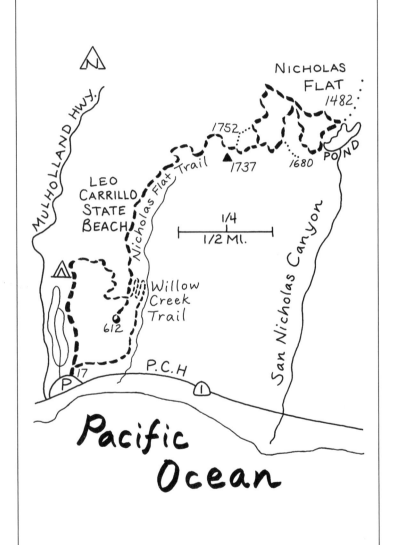

Hike 38: LEO CARRILLO AND
NICHOLAS FLAT

NICHOLAS FLAT
1482

1752

1737

1680

POND

LEO
CARRILLO
STATE
BEACH

Nicholas Flat Trail

MULHOLLAND HWY.

1/4
1/2 MI.

San Nicholas Canyon

Willow
Creek
Trail

612

P.C.H

17

P

1

Pacific
Ocean

⚘LEO CARILLO AND NICHOLAS FLAT
Level 3, Hike 38

A challenging ridgetop connector trail links a split loop with amazing views at Leo Carillo State Beach and a small figure eight through a magical pond-jeweled oasis

DISTANCE: 8.4-mile segmented loop; Elevation change: 1,800 feet
DURATION: 2.75–5.5 hours
NOTES: Dawn–dusk; no pets permitted

DRIVING DIRECTIONS: Take PCH north to Leo Carillo State Beach, just before Mulholland Highway comes down to hit the coast. Turn right into the signed Leo Carillo State Beach Parking Lot, where there is ample day-use parking; $3 fee.

This hike is a real journey for its length, rewarding you with a green and tranquil haven at the top of a grueling climb, and endless ocean vistas on your way back down. To begin, cross back through the parking lot near the stop sign, where directly over the entrance road a wide opening to the Nicholas Flat Trail welcomes you to the first part of your climb, to Leo Carillo Ocean Vista. Pass a sign for the Willow Creek Trail (you'll return on it later) immediately up and into particularly succulent coastal scrub where your eye is drawn to shiny purple and yellow wildflowers even in the fall. To your left you see the campground below you as you rise. Great sycamores, oaks, and eucalypti shelter campers and tents. You begin climbing quite steeply as you veer away from the campground on its attendant hillside. Look back for great ocean views.

Turn right, following the trail and passing by a circular stand of tall laurel sumac with a sheltered clearing in the middle. Looping back toward the ocean, still going uphill, you come to a crossroads at the saddle of the hill. Straight up to your right is the short uphill Ocean Vista Trail, which leads strenuously to an overlook of miles and miles of blue Pacific. Down on your far left is the Willow Creek Trail; take it if you just want to go back down to the beach from here. You'll take this on your return route if you're doing the full hike. To do so, turn left here on the center fork onto the signed Nicholas Flat Trail. This takes you along the extended ridge you see before you. After a while you see a comfortable-looking stone resting spot to your left; it's a nice stopping place for views and secluded picnics. Continue up. To your right is a whole wall of granite, sandstone, and limestone tufted with chamise, resembling a natural dam.

After trudging up the spine of the ridge, bear right through a maze of chamise and buckbrush, continue uphill through denser brush, and skirt the south edge of a canyon finger, then hairpin up to your right, curving left, still going uphill. The chaparral begins to get taller and fuller as you approach Nicholas Flat, with evidence of reeds and papyrus among the usual scrubby suspects. Your way is shaded by scrub oak and chamise. Eventually you come to a sign reading NICHOLAS FLAT TRAIL, with an arrow pointing to your left. On the other side of the sign, you can confirm that you've just climbed about 1,700 feet in 2.2 miles from the campground. Turn left at the signpost. Almost immediately, turn right at the next arrow indicator. The trail dips down for your first respite in quite a while to bear left around a small canyon, toward the flat, with its romantic pond.

You soon come to another crossroads: The Nicholas Flat Trail goes straight through; the Ridgeline to Malibu Springs Trail, to your left, will be the final leg of the crazy little eight you're about to embark on through the flat's woodlands and meadows.

Up here the trail remains even as it curves out slightly toward the ocean then makes a sharp left back toward the mountains. Stately scrub oak mixes with larger protective clumps of coast live oak. Soon, ahead of you and off to your left, you see the peaceful grassy meadow. Along the trail there are a number of welcoming rocks to sit upon if you care to rest, meditate, read, or picnic. As you pass through your first official gamut of tall grass, you approach the next crossroads; the knot in the middle of the eight. Turn right here onto the continuation of the Nicholas Flat Trail. After another few yards you hit another crossroads where you bear left—you'll be returning on the trail to your right.

After curving leisurely around coast live oak, with leggy chamise, scrub oak, and buckbrush lining the way, this trail, too, becomes overgrown with grass for a bit, then heads under a beautiful canopy of oaks as it nears the denser vegetation surrounding the pond and its many feeder springs. Here you hit another crossroads, this one unsigned, where the continuation of the trail on the left fork leads you up to the Nicholas Flat parking lot, accessible from Decker Road. Turn right, with a tall grassland to your right and an overgrown riparian wilderness to your left that becomes denser and denser as you near the tule-shrouded pond. Often misted by fog and full year-round, the pond feels remote and mysterious. There are a couple of well-secluded shore areas off the trail that can be utilized for any number of activities. The grasses and reeds along the shoreline are so tall that you could hide out here for hours if you wished.

Near the end of the pond, hook another right, or walk along the edge of the pond down on the left for a while, and return. You come to a fork where you bear right, in about thirty yards. Head slightly uphill through dense chaparral and emerge at the tie of the eight, then walk straight through on the signed Meadows Trail through stately head-high grasses. This trail leads you ever so slightly uphill across the northeast side of the meadow and into the woods again. If you jut off on one of the spur trails leading straight into the heart of the grasslands, be prepared to get lost on a tangle of go-nowhere footpaths that can be very entertaining. You pass a sign that reads TO MALIBU SPRINGS TRAIL nearly covered by scrub oak off to your right. Go straight through here to a wide opening where the trail curves up to the left. To your right, again nearly hidden by scrub oak, is a sign reading RIDGELINE TO LEO CARILLO AND HIGHWAY 1; TO NICHOLAS FLAT TRAIL.

The last uphill thrust of the trip occurs here, when you climb to skirt a hilltop with the meadowland below you to your left. You rise over two small ridges. The sign along the Ridge Trail tells you to bear left and skirt the next hill instead of going straight up over it, but there is a little trail that does so for those who can't get enough uphill climbing. The rest of us bear left as the sign directs. After several minutes you reach the crossroads to finish the figure eight through the flat. To your right is a brown sign directing you TO LEO CARILLO, HIGHWAY 1. Turn right and follow the ridge back down to the Ocean Vista crossroads that we first met as we came up, going left at the first crossroads and right at the second, following the signs back to Leo Carillo.

As you near the ocean you see the lights of fishing boats flick on in the late afternoon, and tiny surfers in the sun during the rest of the day. When you reach the Ocean Vista crossroads, you again have the chance to go up on the Ocean Vista trail. To finish up, hook a sharp left at this junction, taking the unsigned Willow Creek Trail down to the parking lot.

As you descend you see the many switchbacks of the trail ahead of you falling steeply into the canyon. These are followed by a long, shallow descent toward the ocean, where the trail is so straight for a while that you can meditate on the blue expanse before you as you walk. You begin to curve down here and there, but never get as far as the creek after which the trail was named, far below you and overgrown with impassable brush. Curve right to parrallel PCH back to your starting point.

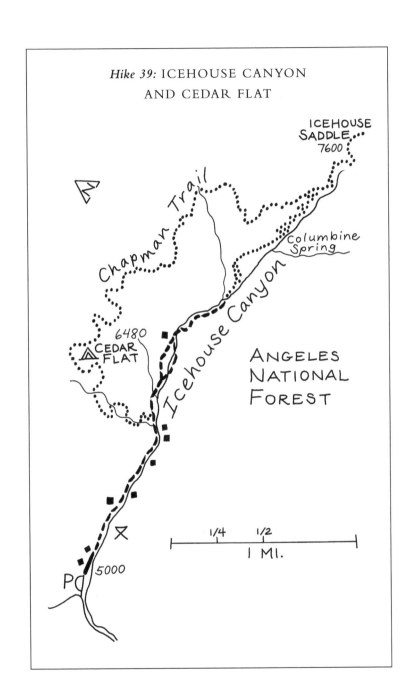

Hike 39: ICEHOUSE CANYON
AND CEDAR FLAT

ICEHOUSE
SADDLE
7600

Chapman Trail

Columbine
Spring

6480

CEDAR
FLAT

Icehouse Canyon

ANGELES
NATIONAL
FOREST

1/4   1/2
1 MI.

5000

PO

ⵌICEHOUSE CANYON AND CEDAR FLAT
Level 3, Hike 39

A steady climb across a rugged granite mountainside to Icehouse Saddle, where trails to five peaks branch off, and down through the playful, water-rich canyon

DISTANCE: 8.2-mile loop; Elevation change: 2,660 feet
DURATION: 3–5 hours
NOTES: Dawn–dusk; dogs on leash permitted

DRIVING DIRECTIONS: Take the 210 Freeway east to its terminus as it blends into the 30 Freeway east, to its terminus at Foothill Boulevard; continue east to a left (north) on Mills Avenue; shallow right to Mt. Baldy Road at first stop sign. Just after passing through Mt. Baldy Village, you will see a well-signed turnoff to your right for Icehouse Canyon. Turn right here, then immediately left into the large, paved lot; no fee.

The trail through captivating Icehouse Canyon starts at the far end of the parking lot to your right, just right of the stone foundation of a long-crumbled building. After a mile in its blissful bed, we'll rise up on the Chapman Trail to climb to Icehouse Saddle—from which most of the Cucamonga Wilderness's major peaks can be reached—then explore the entire canyon on the way back down. As you enter the canyon you are immediately greeted by a continuing veinwork of trails down to shady zones and perfect picnic possibilities along the playful creek, which is lively even during the dry season, creating an always entertaining sequence of multitiered cascades and swirling or calm pools among boulders and thin island arms.

The paved trail soon gives way to a smaller foot trail to your left, away from the creek, and starts heading uphill. You pass by a dilapidated cabin or two near the beginning, and then see that the entire lower canyon is studded with rustic cabins, most of them inhabited (at least during weekends) for the warm part of the year. Alders and sycamores mix and mingle in great shade canopies over the always active stream. After ten minutes or so the trail hairpins up out of the canyon, at probably the best place to go down into the canyon if you wish to hide out in the shady glens for the day. The trail hugs the side of the granite mountain, and gets quite rocky as it climbs over the boulders and shattered rocks that have slid down the mountainside over the years, crossing a series of tributaries that rush or trickle into the creek below.

You soon rise along a wooden railing to cross a cliffside bridge, over another tributary that cascades down to the creek. It's so lush here that wild columbines bloom in the autumn. You go by a whole little community of cabins up at this point, and soon after reach the signed Chapman Trail that branches off on a sharp left on its way to Cedar Glen, a walk-in campsite. As you rise up, check out the granite mountains to the left, with pines and redwoods sticking angularly out of them like toothpicks in a mammoth hors d'oeuvre. This kind of rough, steep, crumbly, haphazardly treed landscape is the hallmark of the Mt. Baldy area. Soon you make a right away from the canyon and head up into the mountains to the north, where the trail makes a nice, graded ascent on railed switchbacks. Here, at around 5,000 feet, you are in the crossing lanes between high desert and mountain flora. Make your way through a manzanita hillside studded by dead sycamores—an eerie wilderness punctuated by the dry exclamation points of yucca whipplei spires.

The trail becomes extremely rocky as you pass across the midpoint of a one-time granite avalanche, and then through a head-high maze of manzanita and chamise to a creek; crossing the creek, the flora can be quite brambly. You pass some interesting burned redwood skeletons up to an open viewpoint where you can look back toward the west to see the San Gabriel Mountains melting out of the canyon beyond you in ever vaguer violet and periwinkle layers into the dusty rose distance. Bluebirds hop and flutter about among the scrub. After a mile and a half on the Chapman Trail you reach Cedar Glen, which is a pack-in/pack-out, permit-only campsite on a wonderful flat at 6,400 feet. A cross breeze blows through the glen during the summer and early autumn months, making it a cool, high-country oasis. There are also copious sidetrails leading off to vista points and hidden cubbyholes.

Wend your way through Cedar Glen and out through the other side on a stone-bordered path accompanied by the rich smell of cedar, and make your way along a plateau through a watershed area, climbing ever so slightly, and then a little more steeply on switchbacks, swinging all the way back out to parallel the canyon, now far below you. You follow a narrow, rocky, sometimes slippery one-track path around steep gorges nearly the entire way to the saddle—this trek is not for the vertiginous. This is a good hike to get you used to the rockiness and the narrow paths of this area before hiking Mt. Baldy (Hike 49), without Baldy's extreme steepness. As you climb, if you look out toward the west you get an even better view of the receding rows of the San Gabriel Mountains, now looking flat and chromatic in their neat, purplish sine wave rows. There's a nice granite climbing alcove to your left (obviously, since there's usually a sheer drop to your right) an hour or more along the Chapman Trail.

The rest of the Chapman Trail is lined with wobbly, slippery granite along the waist of this mountain high above Icehouse Canyon. Heading toward the canyon, you junction with the Canyon Trail for the last half a mile of steep switchbacks to the saddle, a wide and windy open area with a seating log and a well-drawn podium map of the Cucamonga Wilderness showing trails that begin here to its peaks: Ontario, Bighorn, and Cucamonga Peaks, and Timber Mountain, each at just under 9,000 feet.

Return to the Chapman Trail junction from the saddle, and turn left down the Canyon Trail. The sign points nearly straight down, and it's not kidding. You lose about 500 feet in a quarter of a mile on the dizzying switchbacks that lead to the canyon floor. Aren't you glad you didn't have to climb up this way?

Near the bottom of the canyon, you pass a spring to your left, the first sign of the active life of water here. Skirt the plant-choked narrows into the wider part of the canyon. The trail through it is a well-routed, sinewy romp among the canyon's best features—just curvy enough to be interesting. You start out with the creek a trickle among some sturdy, slightly singed cedars and baby sycamores, regrowing from a recent fire.

Crossing a series of small tributary streams, you pass through a collection of huge pieces of granite that have fallen from the hillside up and to the left of you, with amazing striations and designs indicating the jagged happenstance of their breaking points. There is a traditional Japanese and Chinese contemplative art called *suiseki*, which involves gathering the most outrageously beautiful and interesting stones you can find and fashioning pedestals for them, placing them in strategic points around your home as casual departure points into lucid dreaming. Here you see a Southern California–style exhibition of this aesthetically rigorous craft, out under the open sky, its monoliths set at cunning angles in pairs and trios, each a bonafide miracle of form and impact.

Farther down the canyon along the easy-to-follow trail you begin to see foundations of old cabins, with the creek running strongly now over its split-level bouldered bed, creating a series of pools and cascades. Large cedars line your way. You cross a tributary near one of these cascades on a bridge of logs, now well into the denser, lower section of the canyon, where scrub oak and sycamore have joined the redwoods and cedars as they get smaller, giving way to alders.

The rest of the way down a delightful run of leaping waters serenades you. The skyscraping granite convergences rise up above you into sister peaks studded with various firs. Perky paths entice you down many times along the way to take a moment by the creek to listen to its restful run over glass-smooth rocks, dip your feet in the pools, and climb the many huge boulders that have come to rest on its banks. Along with the East Fork of the San Gabriel River on the way to the Bridge to Nowhere (Hike 46) this is the best place in the area to enjoy swimming holes, boulder-hopping, frog chasing, and cascade-side picnicking.

Soon after this you come to the first occupied cabin on your way down; a sweet red shack on a large flat area. You head down into the lower part of the canyon in earnest now, passing the Chapman Trail turnoff. The creek looks different on the way down, as nearly all trails do—even more inviting and full of picnic and hideaway possibilities. Enjoy the bottom of this capacious tree-filled canyon along its final mile, which is a must-explore if you're looking for ways to entertain rambunctious little children.

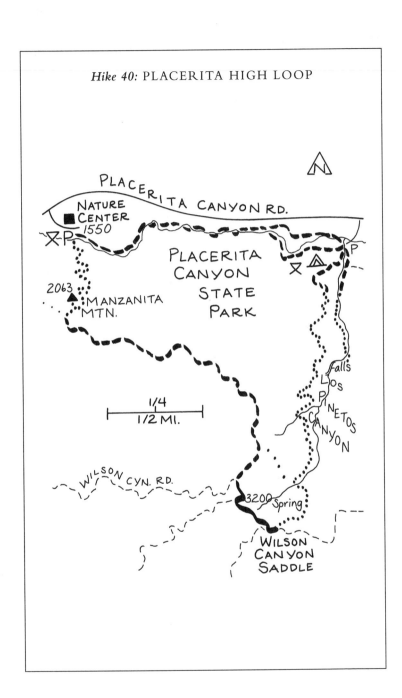

Hike 40: PLACERITA HIGH LOOP

PLACERITA CANYON RD.

NATURE
CENTER
1550

PLACERITA
CANYON
STATE
PARK

2063
MANZANITA
MTN.

1/4
1/2 MI.

Falls

Los
Pinetos
Canyon

WILSON CYN. RD.

3200 Spring

WILSON
CANYON
SADDLE

PLACERITA HIGH LOOP
Level 3, Hike 40

A steep, challenging climb up a barren ridge to a view-rich saddle, then down a twisting canyon to a waterfall sidetrip, and back along rugged Placerita Canyon

DISTANCE: 8.4-mile loop; Elevation change: 2,000 feet
DURATION: 3–5.5 hours
NOTES: 9 A.M.–5 P.M.; dogs on leash permitted

DRIVING DIRECTIONS: Take I-5 north out of L.A. to the northbound 14 Freeway (Antelope Valley Freeway), exit right (east) on Placerita Canyon Road after six-plus miles. After three-plus miles on Placerita Canyon Road, turn left into the well-signed parking lot at the entrance to the park, and follow the graded dirt road to park near the education center; no fee.

Combine the slippery, rocky narrowness of the Chapman Trail in Icehouse Canyon (Hike 39) and the relentless incline to the highest point of the hike on which you are about to embark, and you've got the two major ingredients you need to prepare for the trek up to Mt. Baldy (Hike 49). Cross the creek bed just beyond the education center and take the signed trail toward Manzanita Mountain/Firebreak Ridge, up a set of railroad-tie steps to your left. Climb a rugged hill through prickly chaparral, dip into some shade heading downhill for a bit, then ascend to a crossroads, looking out west toward the Santa Susana Mountains. Up to your right 100 yards is the little bump called Manzanita Mountain, at 2,063 feet, which you can conquer if you must. Your most grueling climb is still to come.

Take the left fork from the trail and begin. You climb relentlessly across a barren ridge to the corner of Whitney Canyon Road at 3,200 feet—the high point in the trip. Try to hike this portion in the morning before the sun becomes too intense. On the way, the trail is unmistakable except at a point where a path to your left rises up to a ridge near the radio towers on the mountains south of you. Veer right here around the last hill toward the towers. At the top, you come to two sets of wooden posts and a dusty plateau. Turn left on the wide dirt road, head over a slight hump, and relish the knowledge that it's all downhill from here.

You curve to the right, past a sign designating multi-use road 3N64, where you bear left; a big yellow sign points toward Santa Clarita with a faded orange arrow. After a few minutes you reach a large crossroads where there is a gate and a bunch of posts off to the right. To your left is a sign reading MULTIPLE USE TRAIL GUIDE-LINES. . . . Make a left here down onto the Los Pinetos Trail into Los Pinetos Canyon. Whitney Canyon Road here turns into the Santa Clara Divide Road and heads back up. Do not go up. You've had enough uphill. Go down to the left on a beautiful, shady trail that zigzags down through oak woodland into the cool canyon. After several minutes you reach a large cistern reading, faintly, LAR-FCP1950 LOS PINETOS. Take a hairpin left here instead of going up to the right. Try to do this hike in the spring, because the area is swarming with gnats in the summer.

At the bottom of the hill you pass another cistern, and take the right fork to see the "Centennial Tree," a 100-plus-year-old coast live oak. You are now in the Walker Ranch Group Campground. For a cool and captivating springtime sidetrip, take a sharp right on the signed Waterfall Trail from the open information board area at the entrance to the campground. As you head back up into the canyon, the trail cuts up to the right on a terraced hillside past a wonderfully healthy specimen of poison oak. The trail soon joins the creek, where you boulder-hop the rest of the way up into the canyon, getting your feet quite wet if the rains have been particularly strong. A sign pointing to the right directs you to the waterfall in the bend of the creek, a dainty little thing that feeds a large rocky bed with a delightful sound reminiscent of a riverboat wheel.

Retrace your steps to the campground, and turn left past the bulletin boards, following the Placerita Canyon Trail past an old fireplace to the right and a fallen tree to the left. Water is available here, and the education center is two miles ahead through the pleasant canyon bottom, sometimes dipping to cross the creek, among scrub oak, yerba santa, and mountain mahogany, with plenty of rustic picnicking sites along the way.

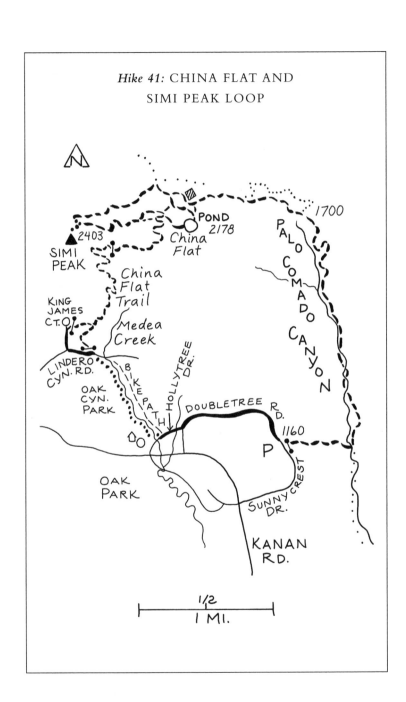

Hike 41: CHINA FLAT AND
SIMI PEAK LOOP

N

1700

PALO COMADO CANYON

POND 2178
China Flat

▲ 2403
SIMI PEAK

China Flat Trail

KING JAMES CT.

Medea Creek

HOLLYTREE DR.

LINDERO CYN. RD.

BIKE PATH

OAK CYN. PARK

DOUBLETREE RD.
1160

P

OAK PARK

SUNNYCREST DR.

KANAN RD.

1/2
1 MI.

❧ CHINA FLAT AND SIMI PEAK LOOP

Level 3, Hike 41

A challenging, entertaining trek through Palo Comado Canyon to China Flat, up to Simi Peak, and back down a rugged hillside through Medea Creek and Oak Canyon

DISTANCE: 10-mile loop; Elevation change: 1,300 feet
DURATION: 3.75–6 hours
NOTES: Dawn–dusk; dogs on leash permitted except in Oak Canyon Park

DRIVING DIRECTIONS: From the 101 Freeway take the Kanan Road exit north two-plus miles to a right (east) on Sunnycrest Drive; the name of the street changes to Doubletree as it curves left (north); park along the curb in this area; no fee.

This variety-filled day-hike at the extreme northwest of the Los Angeles sphere of influence takes you through eight distinct environments: two different canyons, a pond and its marsh, an oak savannah and a southern oak woodland, a rocky peak, a riparian wilderness, and an extreme example of modern Southern Californian suburbia.

Your trip starts out east on a wide dirt path where the signed PUBLIC RECREATION TRAIL begins in an open space past a gate at the far side of the Sunnycrest/Doubletree changeover curve. Stroll through a hilly grassland listening to the rolling chirps of daytime crickets and peering at a small mysterious dome jutting out of the ground to your right. Before you know it, you're far from civilization, beckoned on by soaring hawks and circling crows.

Turn left at the Palo Comado Canyon Trail junction sign, toward Sheep Corral, and head down the dirt road that is a leftover from the ranching era of early last century. The rolling land to the east of you, all the way to Chesebro Canyon, (which you can add to devise a longer loop if you don't mind the annoyance of the sizzling power lines that follow its trail), was bought in 1993 by the Santa Monica Mountains National Recreation Area from Bob Hope, making this super loop possible. The rolling hills between these two canyons, especially as you head into an oak-canopied run-off bed, generically evoke California's golden era (the "pioneer" days), and have been used in various movies and TV shows, including one of my childhood favorites, *Little House on the Prairie*.

Stay on the main dirt road as it zigzags, sometimes strenuously, up into the hills while the canyon falls away below you, though smaller trails may dart off. Some of these lead to the crest that runs along the trail as it bends west and starts an easier climb. Scramble up one and navigate the rocky outcrops of the crest for an expert-level addition to this already challenging loop.

Past these rocks you reach a summit, and descend lightly through lusher brush, past an abandoned corral and rusted engine to China Flat, where a glistening, disused stockpond takes center stage among sage, tall grasses, and rock formations. Follow the little side trail to the pond, where secret places abound, and explore. Many archaeological finds of prehistoric Indian implements have been made in the marsh and boulders that surround the pond and in the hilltop oak savannah beyond.

But before you are enticed by the shade and peace of this savannah, head back to the main trail and take it north, past one fork, where it bends east, then north again. Here you find a triple crossroads. Take the sharp left, which leads you west along the northern edge of the hills to connect with a curving, steep trail the last few hundred treacherous yards up Simi Peak. Take a break here. Have an energy bar. To the north is the enclave of Simi Valley, carved into the verdant bowl below, and almost straight down to the southwest is Oak Park, the upscale country-living suburban community on one of whose streets your car is parked.

Retrace your steps down the curving path, and stay on it as it bypasses a left turn to the path upon which you approached the peak. This takes you back down to China Flat, where you bear right at the first fork and follow the trail in an S-shaped turn as it connects to the China Flat Trail in the oak savannah north of the pond. Stroll west for a bit along this serene trail, which harbors many shady, quiet, secluded spots for picnics, naps, or impromptu yoga sessions.

As you leave the savannah, bear left and pass one more quick summit before heading right, past a couple of buzzing beehives and a rotting fence, onto the main part of the China Flat Trail, which hairpins back and forth down the hills all the way to the outskirts of suburbia on Lindero Canyon Road. Stop and take in the many unique caves, grottoes and miniature thickets that stud your path.

Directly across Lindero Canyon Road, you enter the Oak Canyon Park Nature Trail along Medea Creek—a small, charming riparian wilderness with a variety of trees and birds and enlightening interpretive plaques along the way. Use the dirt path along the creek itself rather than the boring, paved bicycle lane that runs above it, and follow the creek all the way to the entrance of the park, where a couple of duck ponds and a gazebo have been built to entice poolside suburbanites into the wilderness. Here you cut left across the park and up onto Hollytree Drive. You have now entered hardcore suburbia.

Make a left on Hollytree, follow it a couple of blocks, and make another left onto Doubletree. A little over a mile remains, all on well-kept sidewalk, past glittering examples of planned mini-communities and public parks, dotted with disconsolate clans of disaffected teenagers, and laced with speeding housewives and gardeners in SUVs and pickup trucks, to your calmly waiting car.

⚘SOUTH MT. HAWKINS LOOP
Level 3, Hike 42

A steady, steep climb to a pristine peak in the peaceful high country,
through a sparse, high-altitude forest to another peak, and down a portion
of the lovely Pacific Crest Trail

DISTANCE: 11.4-mile loop; Elevation change: 3,400 feet
DURATION: 4–7.5 hours
NOTES: Dawn–dusk; highly inadvisable during winter
months; dogs on leash permitted.

DRIVING DIRECTIONS: From the 210 Freeway in Azusa, take
the 39 Highway exit north several miles, quite winding as it
climbs, and full of fallen rubble, to a right turn into the Crystal
Lake Recreation Area toward the Crystal Lake Campground.
Drive all the way through the campground and park off-street at
the terminus of the paved road near a locked gate at Deer Flats,
where there is a sign designating the Windy Gap Trail to your left;
National Forest Adventure Pass required.

To begin this ambitious climb to two peaks at over 8,000 feet each,
take the signed Windy Gap Trail from the parking area, which is
clearly marked with a stone-bordered path as it winds quickly up
through the campground. At the top you reach a crossroads with a
signed list of possible destinations. Take the South Mt. Hawkins
Lookout Road, turning right on the wide fire road for 3.7 miles of
relentless, unshaded climbing, which you'll want to undertake
before midday.

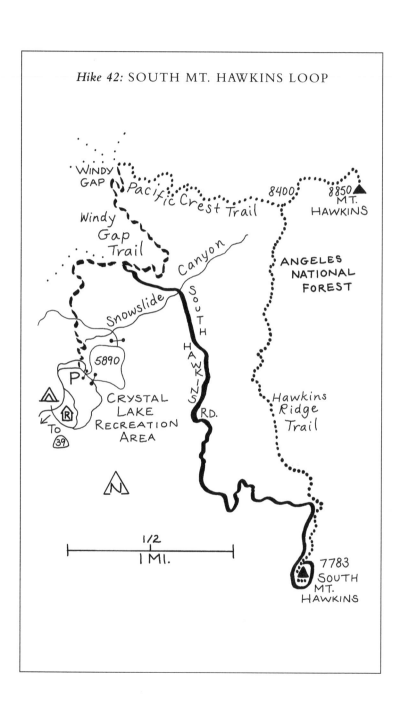

Hike 42: SOUTH MT. HAWKINS LOOP

WINDY GAP

Pacific Crest Trail

8400

8850 ▲
MT.
HAWKINS

Windy
Gap
Trail

Canyon

ANGELES
NATIONAL
FOREST

Snowslide

South

5890

Hawkins
Ridge
Trail

P

HAWKINS

RD.

CRYSTAL
LAKE
RECREATION
AREA

TO
39

Ⓡ

N

1/2

1 MI.

7783
SOUTH
MT.
HAWKINS

As you near South Mt. Hawkins you reach a fork where the fire road heads right to wind lazily up the mountain. Take the more interesting footpath beyond it, going up steeply to the ridge through the forest. The lookout atop the mountain dates from 1906 and is protected as a historic site, soon to be refurbished. This is an excellent place for solitary picnicking and unparalleled views.

Take the same trail back down and continue straight through the junction, north on a short connector to the Hawkins Ridge Trail, a beautifully graded trail that winds through a coniferous forest where the deer are calmer for some reason, less skittish than those you might run across in lower country. The trail continues, dipping down at times but mostly climbing, to a junction with the Pacific Crest Trail, from which you can see the entire Antelope Valley spread before you to the north. To your right, the trail leads quickly up to the crest of Mt. Hawkins, becoming a rough scramble in the last couple hundred yards. Go ahead and bag the peak if you're a mountain-hopper, and return to this point, where you continue down the Pacific Crest Trail. You wind through the sparse forest where the wind blowing through the firs sounds like a fast-moving river. At Windy Gap, your next junction, five trails merge. Make a sharp left down onto the Windy Gap Trail, the only one left unsigned.

Heading earnestly downhill as scrubby, stubborn chaparral takes over from the pines, you soon hit the fire road on which you initially turned to scale South Mt. Hawkins. Cross it, and follow the Windy Gap Trail back through the campground to your starting point.

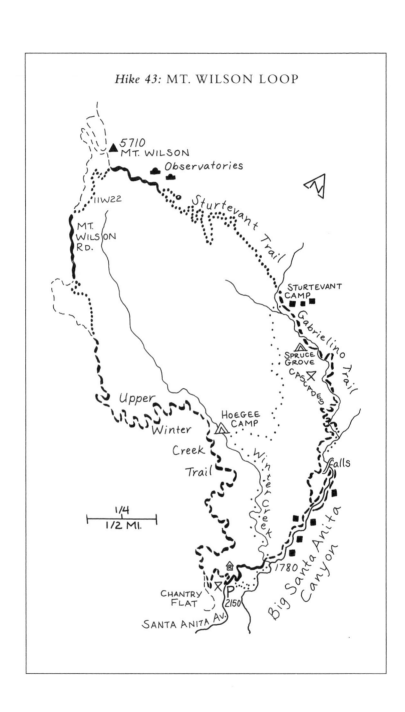

Hike 43: MT. WILSON LOOP

▲ 5710
MT. WILSON

Observatories

11W22

Sturtevant Trail

MT.
WILSON
RD.

STURTEVANT
CAMP

Gabrielino Trail

SPRUCE
GROVE
CASCADES

Upper

HoEGEE
CAMP

Winter

Falls

Creek

Winter Creek

Trail

Big Santa Anita Canyon

1/4
1/2 MI.

1780

CHANTRY
FLAT

P
2150

SANTA ANITA AV.

ꓥ MT. WILSON LOOP
Level 3, Hike 43

A long, demanding climb to the top of Mt. Wilson, with its rich history and observatories, and a challenging trek down gorgeous, lush Big Santa Anita Canyon

DISTANCE: 14-mile loop; Elevation change: 3,930 feet
DURATION: 5–8.5 hours
NOTES: 6 A.M.–10 P.M.; dogs on leash permitted

DRIVING DIRECTIONS: Take the 210 Freeway east from L.A. to Arcadia, exit north at Santa Anita Avenue, and take it all the way up to its gated terminus, steep and winding for the last couple of miles, at Chantry Flat, where there are three large parking lots, a ranger's station, and dozens of widely-spaced picnic tables; National Forest Adventure Pass required.

To begin your trek up Mt. Wilson, with its sentinel tribe of transmission towers and world-famous observatories, find the FIRE ROAD, KEEP CLEAR sign to the left of the ranger station where the road that leads beyond the gate is marked 2N41. Another sign lets you know you are on your way to the Upper Winter Creek Trail, with Hoegees Camp three miles ahead, and Mt. Wilson four miles nearly straight up beyond that. Swing around the chain-link fence and up the paved road that curves around the campground and up through a shady forest. To your right you come to a map of the immediate area, and a sign for the Upper Winter Creek Trail, a dirt path on which you turn right, with Mt. Wilson 6.5 miles ahead.

The first part of this trail is a delightful wind up along the canyon against its walls, now in shade, now in light. As you begin to near Hoegee's Camp after 45–70 minutes, you switchback down into the canyon itself, past a beautiful flat-edged boulder hanging out over the trail, to the signpost at a fork in the road. Going straight will take you to the Mt. Zion junction and Hoegees Camp; Mt. Wilson is 4.5 miles up to your left.

You're going to be climbing three thousand feet in the next 4.5 miles, so pace yourself. Much of this earnest ascent takes place within the next three miles of severe switchbacks to the Mt. Wilson fire road.

You spot some of the buildings of Hoegees Camp down to your right as you head uphill. You may be pleasantly surprised to find that the switchbacks are excellently graded and under the cool shade of oaks, cedars, and redwoods throughout. After over an hour of strenuous climbing, you come to another fork. Hairpinning to your left is a mountain bike/horse trail. A foot-traffic-only trail leads to your right. Since most of the trail is shaded, this is a good summer hike, though it's nicest in the spring when everything's lush, or in the colorful autumn.

When you do reach the sunlight, the view—and how high you have climbed—will astound you. Five miles in you reach the large crossroads to the connector trail leading to the Mt. Wilson Toll Fire Road, with Mt. Wilson right above you, though it's still 2.25 miles to the top. Turn right on this connector trail, continuing uphill to turn right on the Mt. Wilson Road. At the next crossroads, when you see a small cement power station to your left, where this road connects with a larger fire road, look carefully to your right for an unmarked trail that bypasses the rest of the boring fire road all the way up to the top of Mt. Wilson. Turn right at the

grove of four oak trees near a fallen sign reading MT. WILSON TRAIL,
11W22 SIERRA MADRE.

After winding up this trail through tall scrub oak mixed with
stubby firs, you come to a large flat asphalt area atop Mt. Wilson,
with the battalion of radio towers to your left, and the continuation of your trail to your right, including the observatories. Follow
the paved road up, or take the railed walking trail. There are
benches, picnic areas, and even a resting pavilion here atop the
mountain, with various trails leading through them to the observatories. The best walking trail to the observatories is to the south
side, or to your right of the pavilion as you come up. There's a
guided walking tour of the observatories at one P.M. on weekends.
As you walk along the paved road you see a sign reading RIM TRAIL
to the left, and OBSERVATORY AND STURTEVANT TRAIL straight ahead.
The Sturtevant Trail is the one you'll take back down to Chantry
Flat. For now, stop and have a picnic.

The astronomical museum that you pass is open only on
weekends from one P.M. to four P.M. Continue on the paved road
past the solar observatory and the sixty-inch telescope. The trail is
dotted with plaques describing both the telescopes and the natural
features of the area. Continue right at the fork, from which you
can see the main observatory with its immense white dome up to
your left. At the next fork you come to a series of labs and private
drives, with the Sturtevant Trail straight up to your left, as indicated. Another sign at the end of this road, as it curves left to the
100-inch telescope, directs you to turn right at a cabled pole railing, skirting a chain-linked research area. A larger sign invites you
to turn left down the Sturtevant Trail. This initial part of the
Sturtevant Trail is the best area for views, especially if you take the
viewpoint spur before heading downhill, which leads out to a ver-

tiginous railed outlook point, where you can get a 360-degree view of the San Gabriels. Backtrack to the sign for the Sturtevant Trail, turning down the hill as directed.

You enter the shade quite quickly under a forest filled with redwoods and alder. The trail snakes down, sometimes hairpinning (watch for these and don't go off any cliffs), in a cool oak and redwood patchwork, passing some of Southern California's largest and oldest redwoods on the way to Sturtevant's Camp. As you near Sturtevant's, you find yourself strolling along a rambling stream, especially lively during wet months. Eucalyptus and alder take over from redwood here, with some slender aspen mingling in. At the sign, head toward the Gabrielino Trail junction, an eighth of a mile to your left. To your left are the upper reaches of Spruce Grove Camp, with its redwood cabins and stone chimneys.

Shortly after this, the trail goes straight across one of the many dams across the creek, and continues on the other side. Don't miss the sharp right turnoff here; keep going forward into the camp. You head down the opposite side of the creek to another signpost, turning right toward Chantry Flat, four miles ahead. Crossing the stream again, you pass through a creekside picnic ground at Spruce Grove. The lower you go the more gorgeous this riparian wilderness becomes, with large outcroppings of rocks and canopies of green in the spring, or blankets of fallen leaves in autumn, supplied by twisting spruce and tall, slender aspen. You are now well on your way to Sturtevant Falls, an end-of-hike bonus.

Going up and over a few more dams, you eventually descend into the Cascades Picnic Area, where, during the wet season, the water tumbling over the rocks creates quite a show, its glory meekly apparent even during summer and fall. Cross the creek again (quite a task if the cascades are performing) and rise up along the wall of the canyon as the creek falls away in a series of tiny waterfalls. You emerge into the sunlight again high up on the canyon wall. At the Falling Sign Junction take the Upper Falls Trail, which turns a sharp hairpin left down into the canyon.

Pools form here and there as the trail goes down creekside and back up again, skirting rock formations, crossing a log past another dam with a charming green cabin to your right—number 94, the first of a series of privately owned cabins that were once part of an early wilderness resort. Past a stand of slim-leaved Mojave yuccas that look strangely out of place, yet comfortable, under the alders and oaks, you traverse a haphazard collection of large rocks and boulders, some of them perfect for climbing and lounging, to a minor waterfall into a deep blue pool. Another small waterfall precedes the main attraction, Sturtevant Falls, which plummets sixty feet to the canyon floor below, set off by a semicircle of rocks with an audience of oak, aspen, alder, poplar, redwood, and spruce in their own semiprivate vestibule. The cliff that closes off one side of this staging area leads you to the canyon floor. Notice and heed the signs reading NO SHORTCUTTING on the slippery, supersteep slopes that lead down to the floor just below the falls.

To get to the base of the falls, continue down to a junction in the floor below where you turn left on the Lower Falls Trail and head up canyon half a mile to get the full waterfall experience under the splendid play of the spray. Turn around to follow the Falls Trail down through the vast, well-shaded canyon, exploring the creekbed at whim as it beckons.

At the major crossroads, turn right, then left over the bridge to join Santa Anita Road back to Chantry Flat. It's quite a strenuous half-mile trudge up this barren road. For a shadier, but no less strenuous, final leg, take the Falls Trail down to the First Water Trail, a small path that heads right to scale a near-cliff on tight switchbacks to junction with the road just short of the parking areas.

LEVEL 4:

Adventures

Thoroughly challenging, strenuous, and involving hikes for extremely ambitious novices and experts; some trailblazing, rock-climbing, and bushwhacking featured—wild and wooly.

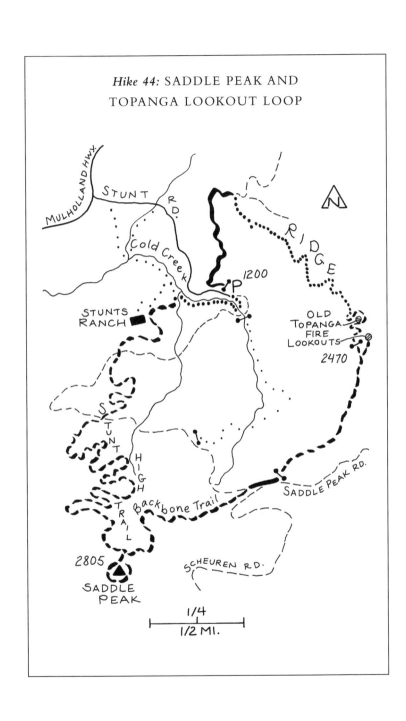

Hike 44: SADDLE PEAK AND
TOPANGA LOOKOUT LOOP

MULHOLLAND HWY.

STUNT RD.

Cold Creek

1200

P

STUNTS RANCH

RIDGE

OLD
TOPANGA
FIRE
LOOKOUTS

2470

STUNT HIGH TRAIL

Backbone Trail

SADDLE PEAK RD.

2805

SADDLE
PEAK

SCHEUREN RD.

N

1/4
1/2 MI.

SADDLE PEAK AND TOPANGA LOOKOUT LOOP
Level 4, Hike 44

A brief paradise of riparian wilderness in Cold Creek, then a steep ascent to Saddle Peak, across to two old fire lookouts, and trailblazing down a tricky, rocky ridge

DISTANCE: 7-mile loop; Elevation change: 1,800 feet
DURATION: 3–5 hours

DRIVING DIRECTIONS: From the 101 Freeway, take Topanga Canyon Boulevard exit south to a right onto Mulholland Drive. Bear left onto Mulholland Highway at the light after one mile; about eight miles to a left onto Stunt Road. Just past the one-mile marker on Stunt Road, there's a wide dirt turnout on the right with a chain-link fence and a bright aquamarine outhouse beyond it. Park in the dirt lot under the faded brown sign for the Stunt High Trail; no fee.

Head through the chain-link fence and down into Cold Creek to begin this adventure, crossing the creek immediately into a gorgeous canyon packed with all sorts of oak and other lush coastal riparian plant life. Cross the creek again and follow it on its left side, noticing what a perfect mini-adventure this first part of your hike would be for children. Water rushes in the creek beside you, and there are various points of entry to the creek itself off to the right. You cross a gulley that features a small waterfall into the creek during wet season, and then another, dipping down to cross an even larger one, and then back up. Just past this lies the best place at which to go down and explore the creek, full of rocks and cascades and trees to climb. The trail then rises above the creek to a fork. To the right you can continue along Cold Creek for another quarter mile, then walk back up Stunt Road to the parking area. For now, you turn left onto the Stunt High Trail.

You quickly emerge from riparian wilderness into scrub oak chaparral as you begin climbing, gently at first. After a few minutes you reach another fork. To the right is the UCLA Stunt Ranch (entry by permission only). Named after Henry and Ethel Stunt, its original owners, the 67-acre Stunt Ranch is now a natural preserve and research facility. The Stunt High Trail (open to the public) continues to your left as a small footpath. Cut across a field where, to your left, there was a wasp study in progress last time I did this hike, with white chambers that looked like combination beeboxes and birdhouses studding the meadow. Climb up lazy switchbacks through scrub oak and manzanita, and before long you see Stunt Road below you to your left. Cross the Stunt Ranch Road and follow on the other side as signed. Shortly after, you reach Stunt Road. Turn right and follow it for about fifty yards. The trail continues, unsigned, just after a phone pole reading 1024915H on its metal placard. That's just past mile marker 1.94 on the left side of the street.

Dip in left on the trail, which continues up a set of stone stairs. Most of your climbing comes in the next mile or so, though the grade is so perfect you hardly notice it. Your way is shielded by high hedges of all the major chaparral plants, with sporadic views of the canyons below and mountains above if you've luckily missed the fog that prevails in this area. About forty to sixty minutes into your hike, you reach 2,000 feet, crossing Stunt Road again to your right, where you see a bright orange arrow in the road about thirty yards down on the left side of the street. Here you find a small gate to the left with a sign reading BACKBONE TRAIL TO PIUMA ROAD, 3.2 MILES. You connect with the Backbone Trail here, but branch left very shortly toward Saddle Peak rather than Piuma Road. After five to ten minutes you come to a T-intersection, taking the left turn to Saddle Peak. You climb 800 feet in the next 1.3 miles, on crazy switchbacks through tall chamise, passing through a delta circled by eucalypti and oak a short way beyond the fork, and continuing up to your left. The trail climbs more precipitously, using the bare sandstone of the mountain as natural stairwells here and there.

Soon you find yourself facing a whole wall of sandstone. To your right, various formations that look like something out of a mythical Dr. Seuss setting dot a meadow along with seasonal ponds. The trail takes you right through this amazing sandstone formation show, with lots of entertaining climbing available on the soft, shapely boulders. This meadow is worth the whole hike, even if you hate going uphill. Try to traverse this sandstone flat slowly, peering in caves here and there, climbing in and out of openings between rocks, and using smaller rocks as stepping stones, along another sandstone wall with little cubby holes carved in it. It's the perfect place to drink in every detail.

You then continue up, with views of the valley to your left. Soon after this sight, a small, unsigned trail to your right leads around the back of Saddle Peak and onto its wide, flat apex at 2,805 feet—an excellent view opportunity. Coming back down to rejoin the trail, you turn right, going straight ahead if you wish to skip the peak. More beautiful sandstone formations continue to line your way, each more enticingly climbable than the next. Head downhill around an immense pale beige water tank, then past the beige fence down the asphalt driveway on the other side. Across the street, follow the sign for the continuation of the Backbone Trail, which lets you easily down onto Stunt Road, just near a white "100" painted on the asphalt. Turn right and walk up about twenty yards to the stop sign at the triple intersection of Scheuren, Stunt, and Saddle Peak Roads, heading straight through toward the yellow pipe gate. Continue on the fire road beyond the gate to Topanga's two old fire lookouts, both now defunct.

The road soon becomes paved, sporting some of the most puckish and intriguing graffiti in Los Angeles, most written in stylized hippie-inspired script; my favorite is TRUST YOUR BASIC FUNCTIONS scrawled fire-engine red. The most recent lookout is just above you in all its dilapidated future-of-yesteryear glory, like a set from some postapocalyptic B-movie. It's not very nice, and it's a frequent dumping spot for trashy partiers. Visit it if you feel compelled to do so, then take the dirt road that leads down left from the paved service road past a bent, rusted pipe fence that's propped open by a rock.

Pass through a wide wash with the lookout almost directly behind you. A sandy rise takes you close to a ridge to your right, then downhill. Before the road curves earnestly down to the right, you reach a small sandstone formation and a hilltop—heavily graffitied and partied upon—which houses the ruined foundation of the older Topanga fire lookout. It's a bizarre little platform, completely covered in unintelligible slogans, worthy of the short but strenuous sidetrip. A flurry of little stairways that lead nowhere make it resemble a DiChirico painting. Skirt the lookout mound, and take in the beautiful views of the canyons and ravines below you to your right.

Soon after this, the road becomes a gulley for a while, leading between scrub oak and looping around downhill, past an ultrasmooth sandstone hillside that looks like an entire fossilized blue whale. Sandstone columns to your left, a small one and a large one, watch over you like totems of a lost culture.

The trail abruptly ends at a hilltop clearing full of sandstone formations. Go to the far side of the clearing, and look closely for a little footpath next to a formation of a slightly grayish color that swoops up into a flat point, like a seal's upturned, ball-balancing nose. You can see that this hard-to-find path leads out to the next formation. This is the beginning of your off-trail ridgetop traipse, the penultimate leg of your loop. The wayward way branches off into multiple options, sometimes seemingly impossible to find, and rather treacherous, with some mild rock-climbing along the way. Well-trodden areas show the path of others. You may find yourself doing some light bushwhacking through coastal scrub, and quickly realize it is completely up to you to navigate your own best way over the sporadic rock formations, which are all quite easy to manipulate, with very evident footholds and stepping spaces. It's actually not that difficult, though it may seem so at times. The "path" becomes easier to follow as you go, though it may take you up to an hour to traverse the ridge. Don't rush, and take time to enjoy the views when you stop, probably frequently, in order to strategize your next ten or twenty yards.

Before long the edge of the ridge shimmers into sight, with fire roads running all around below you. Having polished off the sandstone portion of the ridge, you reach a grassland saddle, which you cross to rise to the next hilltop on what is now a very easily distinguishable footpath. Take a rest at the top of the hill, looking back to take in the impressive perspective of the rugged spine you just crossed. The trail continues down a nearly barren hillside to the fire road below. Take any of the final spurs down to the road, and turn left at a triple crossroads with a bench. The road up and to your shallow right goes to Calabasas Peak, and the sharp right curves down into Red Rock Canyon Park, both worthwhile extra trips if your stamina holds up. Wend your way down an easy third of a mile on the fire road to exit around a locked gate just above Stunt Road, your car just ahead of you across the street.

⚘ELYSIAN PARK
URBAN ADVENTURE
Level 4, Hike 45

A full, rambling, demanding tour of this sprawling park in downtown L.A., home to the Dodgers, the L.A. Audubon Society, and various urban-bred wildlife

DISTANCE: 8-mile fractured loop; Elevation change: 800 feet (up and down all the way)
DURATION: 2.5–4.5 hours
NOTES: Dawn–dusk; dogs on leash permitted

DRIVING DIRECTIONS: From the 101 Freeway in downtown L.A., take the Broadway Street exit north through Chinatown. At the unpopulated 1500 North block of Broadway, just before a deco bridge crossing the L.A. River, and just after a glimpse of the Portola Trailhead to the left, turn left onto Park Row Drive and park immediately, curbside; no fee.

Here's a hearty, varied ramble around L.A.'s much-maligned downtown park that throws the surreal juxtaposition between the wild urban and even wilder natural elements of the city into sharp relief. Most Angelenos only hit Elysian Park for the occasional Dodgers game, though it is heavily used locally by cruisers, partiers, vagrants, and junior high school sports teams. Surrounded by the busy city and its clogged freeways, with frequent hazy views of the towers about City Hall, Elysian Park is a wilderness within

Hike 45: ELYSIAN PARK
URBAN ADVENTURE

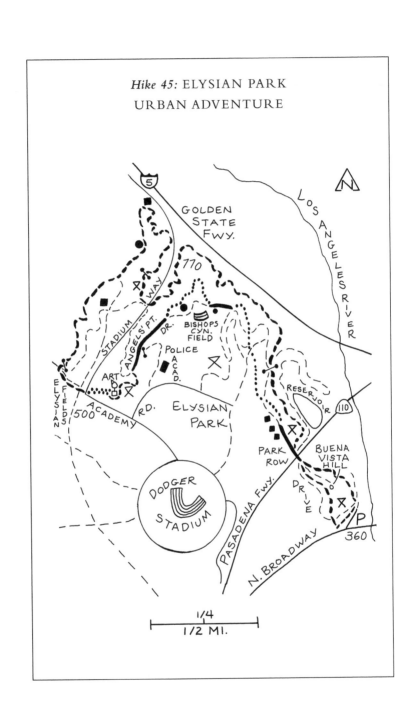

a wilderness that is, if not relaxing, intriguing to explore and experience.

Head back out to Broadway to catch the beginning of the trail, which starts on the sloping hill containing the "1769" plaque, a monument explaining that Don Gaspar de Portola was one of the first colonizers of California, and that he and Fra Francisco Serra, mastermind of the missions, camped here in the summer of that year on route to Monterey, mistakenly passing it and making a great discovery—San Francisco Bay.

You see a sign for the Portola Trail, Historical Landmark #655, here to your west, and begin uphill on the paved trail. Paralleling Park Row Drive at first as the trail ascends, you cross the street, go up the paved drive and make a right to continue uphill beside a stone wall to your left. As you rise, views of the city fall at your feet. Continue to your right at the next fork, staying on the main trail that parallels the street and river far below you. There are many little trails crisscrossing back and forth through this area to the upper tiers of the park all the way to Buena Vista Hill, which will constitute the last leg of our return journey on this boomerang-shaped loop.

As the trail descends toward the river, make a left at your first convenience, toward some eucalyptus and California black walnut trees, up to the next main trail, where you turn right. This trail bends around on the halfway point of the hillside. Soon you see a couple of wooden staircases with metal railings. Go up either one and turn right. Ahead of you is a stop sign, and just above you is a picnic area along the continuation of Park Row Drive. Head straight through the intersection and cross the bridge ahead of you over the Pasadena Freeway, with views of the downtown skyline to your left. Turn right on Grandview Drive just over the bridge through the grassy picnic area, and pick up the far dirt footpath nearest the street going up the opposite hillside. This leads you across a hilltop through eucalyptus, oak, walnut, pine, and palm trees, including a few indigenous varieties. This area—and in fact the whole park—was dedicated in 1940 by the Audubon Society as a bird sanctuary. To your right is the reservoir, which shines a deep cobalt blue in the glinting sun. Continue on the dirt trail along the hilltop to hook up with a wider dirt trail on which you make a shallow right.

At this point you enter the most tranquil part of the park. You can see the lofty eucalyptus tufts burbling in the breeze above you straight ahead as you leave the sound of traffic behind. The chatter of birds greets you.

The trail curves gently uphill through eucalyptus, oleander, and walnut, with plenty of sidetrails down to hidden knolls and thickets, and then curves north to cross winding Park Row Drive again. You can look down upon the Golden State Freeway (I-5), the desolate industrial wasteland far below you, and the hills of Highland Park directly across the river. Cross the street, where our trail continues, swinging around the white gate and continuing to your left. A few moments later, take one of the sidetrails up to the hillock above you, if you like, to get a feeling for how steep and undevelopable most of this park remains, and back down. The main trail continues to your right at the midway point between the treetops and the freeway. You see tons of trash and bits of unidentifiable, broken things along the way, wondering how it all got up here.

Bend left and hook around a ravine away from the freeway, then back again, continuing along the waistline of the hill. Aren't you happy you aren't in that packed freeway down there? Soon after the ravine, you trundle over a treacherous group of rocks and loose dirt clods; then the trail heads down to merge with another one slightly below you, on which you make a shallow left to continue in the same direction. You quickly rise up and turn left along the hillside to parallel Stadium Way, below you to your right, flanked by beautiful green plots of grass, unlike the neglected hillsides which you are currently passing through. As you continue away from the freeway along Stadium Way, you may run across some rather lavish homeless setups, some complete with closet space, separate sitting room, and curtained changing area. You are urged along by the cries and laughs of sports-playing children below you.

At Angel's Point Drive you pass through a gate and cross Stadium Way toward a sign reading GRACIE SIMONS LODGE. Beyond the sign and across the lawn you see another white gate with a green sign next to it, where the trail continues. You wind back down toward the freeway along this trail, where many local junior high school cross-country and track teams train in the fall and spring. Keep to the right to avoid being run into if you should happen upon a herd of them barreling down the trail on a 5k run.

At a sharp hairpin left up the hill and away from the freeway you come to a stone wall, beyond which lies a strange tropical garden and a dilapidated abandoned stylistic mess of a modern house, stranded alone on the hillside above the freeway. Up the hill, you seem to be walking straight into a neighborhood that the trail bends around to your left at the last minute, then to the right on its way toward a pale green water tower. Right after it you reach a charming miniature garden with a bench that is perfect for meditation. This is the Marion Harlow Memorial Grove. Go through the garden and then to your right, or bear right on the main trail around the garden. Stay high up on the hill and avoid the many trails leading down to your left. At ten o'clock is the Los Angeles skyline, and below you to your left is the Gracie Simons Lodge, where weddings and other ceremonies take place. Lithe, small willows and eucalypti line your way. Quail and coyote whir and yap in the hillside up to your right.

Next you descend to a gate; slip past it and cross the outlet street and the main street beyond it, then turn left at the footpath that skirts the wide "Elysian Fields"—a huge grassy area with walnut, oak, pine, and palm trees evenly spaced throughout to define private shade, napping, and stretching areas. At the end of the Fields, you descend down to Stadium Way again. Cross it to get to Academy Drive. Standing on the corner of Academy Drive where it makes a sharp curve left, facing north toward Dodger Stadium, survey the tall, brittle scrub-covered hill just ahead of you, and the monstrous metronomelike object at its apex, its moving metal parts flashing sharp rays of sunlight. You must get a closer look; you must see what it is.

Cross the street, catty-corner, toward the green Gracie Simons Lodge sign. At the double arrows reading ONLY and OK in a yellow diamond on a granite lightpost, scramble up the hillside to find a trail. After a short, treacherous climb through soft dirt, keeping your eye on the spinning silver disc, your way is led by lavender butterflies. The trail gets a bit overgrown and thorny near the top, where a small grassy plateau welcomes you to the backside of what is now revealed to be a complicated piece of civic art—a mechanical extravaganza by Peter Sheier in honor of Frank Glass and Gracie Simons, longtime protectors of the park, which was first dedicated in 1886. The sculpture dates from 1994, and doesn't look as though it will stand the test of time as well as the park has. To your right is Dodger Stadium, a far more secure monument.

Head straight across the sculpture-bearing hillock toward the green, grassy picnic area, bearing left around it on the dirt perimeter. You pass the first steep offshoot to your left to the more shallow central offshoot, straight ahead, which sweeps you gently up to an even better view of Dodger Stadium. Continue to your left, turning left as the road sweeps up. You come to a gate and a paved road, upon which you turn right, continuing through two white poles on either side and past a gated driveway leading down to your right along the palm-lined street, heading toward another pale green water tower ahead of you. Before you curve around the street toward the forest-green pavilion to your right, look off to your left to spot a silver pipe gate with a dirt path leading off beyond it. Go around the gate and along the path, passing behind the water tower with a tall row of palms to your left. Now you are returning toward the river, which you soon make out far below.

Pass the Bishop's Canyon Little League field and head down into a parking area across the street from it. Continue on the trail, which leads away from the gated field, through some chaparral to a stand of five eucalypti, the farthest specimen perfect for climbing or sitting in to watch the city pass in its hurried frenzy below you. Turn right at this eucalyptus onto a very small but well-trodden footpath through the chaparral, high above the first trail you initially took paralleling I-5. This brings you back down to the street that curves around Bishop's Canyon, on which you turn left, following it past a pipe gate and the farther practice field. Below you to your right is a large grassy picnic area with a playground. The street curves to your left as you pass through another gate, where you hit the corner of Angel's Point Drive and Angel's Point Drive, marveling briefly at the concept of a street that crosses itself.

Continue to your far left, not snaking down to the right into the grassy area. At the end of the retaining wall to your left you take some steep steps worn into a rock that lead up to a trail traversing a high ridge affording views of the entire northern sector of Los Angeles. Bear right at the crossroads atop the hill at the eucalyptus bearing indecipherable red and black graffiti. Just down to your left is the street you crossed after taking the reservoir trail toward the freeway. Head straight through toward the center trail on the right. Far down to your left, the reservoir appears. Keep to the top of the ridge on this narrow footpath, and you soon find yourself heading steeply down to a paved crossroads. The sign ahead of you reads ELYSIAN RESERVOIR, POINT GRANDVIEW: LEFT; BUENA VISTA AREA, NORTH BROADWAY ENTRANCE: STRAIGHT AHEAD. Head straight through toward the Buena Vista hilltop path and picnic area.

Follow the paved road past the grassy peninsula toward another white pipe gate with a sign announcing Park Row Drive to your left. Past the next white pipe gate to your left, you see a dirt path leading off beyond you with scars of asphalt along it. Go between the gate and the stubby cemented pipes here to follow this path, veering off from the paved road to your left. This path soon rejoins the main paved road, where you make a shallow left. The spire of City Hall juts up over the hill ahead and to your right. Pass through a gate and follow a short stretch of residential street to cross the same bridge over which you initially crossed the Pasadena Freeway. Bear left at the sign reading BUENA VISTA HILL, following either the paved street or the tangle of narrow paths up and to your left. Continue over the hill taking any route you wish to the grassy slope along Broadway where you began this invigorating, if a bit startling, adventure through the inner city wilds.

✻THE BRIDGE TO NOWHERE
Level 4, Hike 46

Incessant fording and occasional trailblazing up the wild East Fork of the San Gabriel River to an awesome deco bridge on the remains of a lost highway

DISTANCE: 10 miles round trip; Elevation change: 800 feet

DURATION: 3.5–6 hours

NOTES: Dawn–dusk; dogs on leash permitted

DRIVING DIRECTIONS: From the 210 Freeway in Glendora, just east of Azusa, take the Grand Avenue exit north; 3.5 miles to a right on Sierra Madre Avenue; 4.5 miles to a left on Glendora Mountain Road; about twenty miles up this steep and twisting road, bearing left as Glendora Ridge Road splits off to the right, to Glendora Mountain Road's terminus just past where East Fork Road begins at a hairpin left; continue a few hundred yards to a large dirt parking lot on the left with a small ranger station. Fill out a self-issuing wilderness permit at the station; National Forest Adventure Pass also required.

Though it can get too hot for some, summer is the best time to enjoy this upriver trek to the most remarkable hidden monument to L.A.'s determination to connect all parts of its far-flung self against nature's strong objections. The simple, graceful bridge at the end of this hike was as far as builders in the 1930s got in creating a highway from the San Gabriel Valley to the high desert before

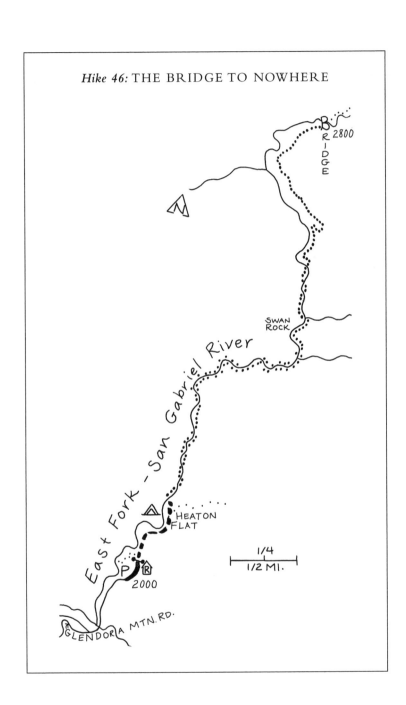

Hike 46: THE BRIDGE TO NOWHERE

BRIDGE 2800

SWAN ROCK

East Fork - San Gabriel River

HEATON FLAT

P R 2000

1/4
1/2 MI.

GLENDORA MTN. RD.

it was destroyed by a huge flood in 1938. Scar tissue of the old road can be seen all the way through the East Fork, which is one of the strongest, fastest, and coldest canyon streams in the Los Angeles area, but the bridge is intact—nearly pristine, in fact—and though manmade, seems a natural wonder. It spans the river just as the mountains on either side close in to create a steep and forceful narrows. At the foot of the narrows you'll find the best sunning rocks and splashing pools in Los Angeles.

This brings me back to summer. You will ford the East Fork numerous times on your way to the bridge and back, which, even in high summer, can leave you soaked to the knees—be sure to wear appropriate shoes. In the spring, the river is often far too swollen from snow runoff to navigate unless you are a diehard daredevil. As the weather cools in autumn toward winter the crossings are far too frigid, and you will smack yourself for not being able to take advantage of the many fine swimming holes that have formed in the river along the way.

As you begin your journey, heading past the ROAD CLOSED sign and following the dirt road to Heaton Flats Campground, the river appears below you to your left. This will be your home for the next several hours. Passing straight through the Heaton Flats Campground along the river on the pair of trails that lead to various low-lying swimming holes, you may be dismayed by the crowds, but you will see as you go along that few of the casual walkers and river revelers actually make it all the way out to the bridge.

A quarter mile up the river, make your first crossing near a jumble of cement girders, part of the evidence of the old highway that will appear here and there throughout the hike. There is a trail here—or rather a system of trails all pushing toward the same goal, but they are unmarked. You will have to keep a close eye out for the connectors and fordings and canyon-wall paths that vein the entire riverbed, crossing the sometimes daunting flow again and again as the canyon narrows, widens, narrows again, then finally opens up into a wide, rocky, yucca-studded wash as it curves to the left (south). Here, the trail rises up the wall of the canyon to your right to follow the route of the old highway the rest of the way to the bridge.

As you near the bridge the trail curves right, the river now rushing far below you. Pass through a small patch of private property that is part of ongoing private gold mining concerns, once profitable, now merely for hobbyists, that still are run in the canyon. The bridge appears before you like a mirage, shimmering at first, then solidifying, showing its age through the slight crumbling of its railings, but regal in its splendor of survival. It is just a bridge, of course, even if it does have a particularly breathtaking arch and sweep to it, but there tends to be a sanctuarylike ambience here, causing even the loudest and chattiest of hikers to observe a few moments of thoughtful silence as they pause to look upriver, then down, in the center of the span.

Beyond the bridge the trail gets narrow and slippery on its way up into the narrows. Climb down one of the various trails to the river below, where there are at least half a dozen boulder and swimming hole arrangements that can comfortably harbor small groups of picnickers and swimmers, far from the noisy and crowded swimming holes near the bottom of the canyon.

In previous hikes, I have noted how a trail can look and feel distinctly different depending on the direction you are traveling. This trip through the East Fork of the San Gabriel River is an extreme example of that phenomenon. The way back from the bridge, though it follows the same route as the approach, takes on such a surprisingly changed atmosphere that it almost feels like a loop hike. Now that you've reached your goal, explore the riverbed more carefully, take some time to notice its rock formations and shady woodlands, catch a frog and let it go, find a secret hiding place, and wiggle your toes in the water. You return to civilization all too soon.

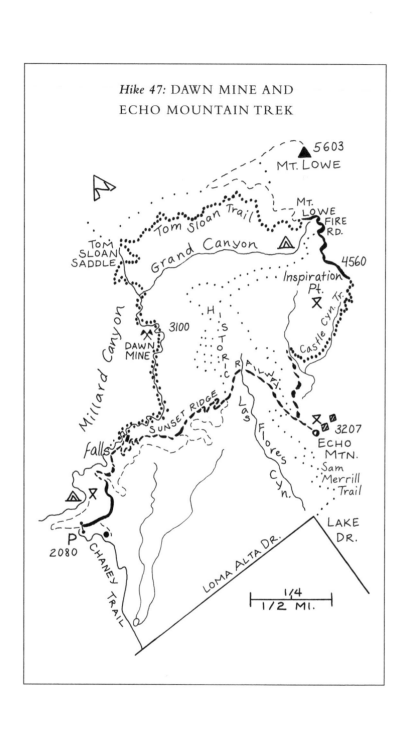

Hike 47: DAWN MINE AND
ECHO MOUNTAIN TREK

5603
MT. LOWE

Tom Sloan Trail

Grand Canyon

MT.
LOWE
FIRE
RD.

TOM
SLOAN
SADDLE

4560

Inspiration
Pt.

Castle Cyn. Tr.

HISTORIC

3100

DAWN
MINE

Millard Canyon

RAILWAY

SUNSET RIDGE

Las Flores

Cyn.

Falls

ECHO
MTN.
3207

Sam
Merrill
Trail

P
2080

CHANEY TRAIL

LAKE
DR.

LOMA ALTA DR.

1/4
1/2 MI.

✄DAWN MINE AND ECHO MOUNTAIN TREK
Level 4, Hike 47

Trailblazing and bushwhacking up wild Millard Canyon, across a ridge to another Inspiration Point, and down through the ruins of a late nineteenth-century resort and railway

DISTANCE: 12-mile loop; Elevation change: 2,800 feet
DURATION: 5–8 hours
NOTES: 6 A.M.–10 P.M.; dogs on leash permitted

DRIVING DIRECTIONS: Take the 210 Freeway to exit north on Lake Boulevard in Altadena, just east of Pasadena. Follow Lake to its terminus to turn left on Loma Alta Drive, then right on Chaney Trail, to its terminus. Turn right to a dead end at a locked pipe gate and park off-street; no fee.

As you head past the locked pipe gate to your right at the end of Chaney Trail, you find a plaque containing an interpretive map of the Mt. Lowe Railway and the hiking trails in the immediate area. This challenging and varied full-day loop detailed here takes you on a serious trek up the wild reaches of Millard Canyon, easily across to Inspiration Point on the Mt. Lowe Fire Road, and then down Castle Canyon to the most striking and informative site along the old Mt. Lowe Railway. Echo Mountain is the ruins of a high-country resort that once included two hotels, a ballroom and casino, tennis courts, private residences, gardens, a power plant, an observatory, and a zoo.

The railway and resort were the fruit of one Thaddeus Sobieski Constantine Lowe's visionary and capitalistic dreams, though—like Lowe's earlier cross-country ballooning adventure that ended unceremoniously when his craft came to land in the middle of a Civil War battle in Virginia—Echo Mountain's lavish resort burned to the ground after only a few years of high-style service in the late 1890s. The railroad continued running to Ye Olde Alpine Inn, a more informal complex a few miles farther up toward Mt. Lowe, and finally took its last run in 1937 under the auspices of a preservation committee. The remains of the railway and resort are well marked throughout; the displays on Echo Mountain and the Sunset Ridge will tell you everything you might want to know about this outlandish, quixotic undertaking, of the type Los Angeles and its constant influx of California dreamers have always been famous for.

Beginning on the road past the gate, curve left and skirt high above lush Millard Canyon, perhaps spotting tents or smoke signals in the campground among the oaks and pines far below. You skirt an arm of the canyon near one of its intense, sharp rock walls. After several minutes you see the Sunset Ridge Trail, your return route, forking off to your right. Continue to your left down into the canyon, crossing a rickety metal bridge past a little brown cabin. Nearly immediately, you descend directly into the canyon, with the main trail leading to the right through the creek bed, and a smaller trail to your left branching off down the canyon to the top of the falls. This ten to fifteen minute detour is well worth the extra time and effort. The coolness and lushness of the canyon are almost overwhelming, and the top of the falls is a daunting collage of climbable boulders that filter water through their gaps. There are plenty of rustic picnicking possibilities here. Backtrack your way to the turnoff point. To continue up the creek, climb up to the trail, turn left, and dip immediately down to the left into the creek bed.

You cross the creek several times, using the bed itself as a trail through a series of cascades and pools. It's a lovely canyon lit by mellow, dappled sunlight through alders. The trail meanders along the creek, hardly noticeable at times, but always there just around the bend. You step over plenty of fallen trees, getting your feet quite wet during spring months. The trail turns to pure dirt as it passes a dam and runoff fixture, going slightly uphill to your left. Interesting for both eyes and feet, the route demands extreme vigilance and, sometimes, ingenuity. White paint marks on various trees and rocks indicate your way.

At a point where a rusted metal pipe crosses the trail as you head up on the right side of the creek, take the trail immediately left (down) or you'll get stranded on a high rocky ledge. From this point on, the trail becomes even more difficult to follow, and the canyon itself is steep, climbing over 2,000 feet to Tom Sloan Saddle, your next reconnaissance point.

Forty to seventy minutes into your hike, you make your way around a large tumble of boulders. If you can find it, the trail rises very steeply out of the creek at this point, to your left. Here the canopy of the canyon opens up to reveal the mountains above. Continue in the rocky bed of the creek to another place where the trail shoots steeply up to the left beside an oak tree clinging with all its life to a rocky bank. Follow the creek itself past a stunted, regrowing sycamore on your right, then a large alder, where the trail climbs steeply up to your right. Here it becomes more manageable, to a point where it crosses the creek toward a rocky hillock surrounded by oak. Just beyond this you spot a tiny door carved into the bottom of the mountain ahead of you. This is the rear adit for the old Dawn Mine, the other side of which you'll encounter farther on.

You cross the creek on the trail among some rugged rocks. If you continue to follow the creek you'll reach an impassable cleft in the canyon. You step out onto a flat arrow-shaped boulder as you cross the creek for the second time, enmeshed in a small wilderness of pools and alders, and look back to see that the trail heads off uphill, skirting the sheer face of the canyon cliff over the large promontory housing the adit. Here the trail zigzags steeply from side to side of the canyon to skirt the impassable rocky places in the bed. Follow the bed around a narrow curve where you see the rusty leftover works of the Dawn Mine up and to your left on the other side of the promontory you skirted earlier. The trail crosses the creek and goes steeply up its left bank, over a crag as the canyon makes another turn. From this point on, sporadic orange dots painted on rocks and trees mark your way. Continue along a slippery, canyon-wall trail on the left bank as the creek falls away below you, then down into the bed once more, reaching a place where two large trees have fallen, crossing the trail. As a note, if a log on this trail does not have a foot-sized notch cut into it, it's acting as a barrier, and not meant to be stepped over.

Follow the larger tree down along a barely perceptible trail, then cross the creek and rise out sharply on the other side, reassuring yourself you're in the right place with the orange dot at the bottom of the creek. Here the trail passes through a thick sycamore copse, with redwoods and cedars beginning to appear. You come to another log, this one with a notch in it. Step through the notch and continue on a now easily followable trail that hairpins right, up and out of the canyon. Millard Canyon becomes more slippery and impassable from this point on.

You rise on a couple of switchbacks. A cleanly sawed log seems to be sliding down the hill, just about to cross the trail, but you see it's stuck that way, suspended in a perpetual state of falling. Soon the crowded canyon foliage thins for a look at the steep, rocky slopes of the Arroyo Seco Front Range. Candlestick plants dot the mountainside trail, which goes up an armlet of the canyon to dip down and cross a tributary. From the other side you get a great view of the canopy from under which you recently emerged. Now heading into dense chaparral, you cross another tributary and notice shapely small firs beginning to dot the trail. You continue to wind up the mountain quite steeply with gorgeous views ahead at every turn.

Eventually, two to three-and-a-half hours into your trip, you reach the Tom Sloane Saddle, signified by four trail signs and a four-pronged oak. Brown Mountain is up and to your left; a shortcut to the Mt. Lowe Fire Road is up and to your right. Take the sharp right around the oak onto the Tom Sloane Trail; the Mt. Lowe Fire Road is 1.8 miles ahead. Here you continue along a rocky, narrow, sometimes slippery but easy-to-follow trail with great views. Clumps of chamise, laurel sumac, buckbrush, and manzanita hug the trail, sometimes overgrown to the point of bushwhacking. You approach several brittle rocky points from which you can overlook the twisted, overgrown canyon below.

After thirty to fifty minutes on the Tom Sloane Trail you start to see the telephone poles and wires on Mt. Lowe Fire Road up and ahead of you. The trail rises steeply on a slippery oak hillside to the road, where you turn right. It's a relief to be on flat ground with more than six inches on either side of you. You make a couple of wide, lazy curves, and bypass a cement runoff that looks like it would be really fun to slide down. The Mt. Lowe East Trail splits off to your left here, and the Mt. Lowe Trail camp is down to your right. Several hundred yards beyond this you reach a large plateau of crossroads where the Sam Merrill Trail to Echo Mountain begins to your right. Continue slightly farther up the road, bending left to Inspiration Point, where a sign beside a canopied platform welcomes you to this

"World Famous Telescope View Overlooking 3,000 Square Miles."
On the other side of the retaining wall telescopes are rigidly pointed
toward various locations: Glendale, Redondo Beach, San Pedro, etc.;
a fun diversion when the air is clean, though smog often impedes the
views. On extremely clear days after rain, you can spot Catalina
Island from here, seventy-five miles to sea.

Just beyond Inspiration Point, the marked Castle Canyon Trail
splits down to your right. Echo Mountain is two miles ahead, and
your starting point is four miles beyond that. Entering fragrant
chaparral, you switchback down into the canyon. The narrow and
slippery trail will be nothing new to you on this trip. After a while
the canyon falls away very steeply below you to your left as you
hug the wall far above it. Shortly after, you cross the creek at the
site of a gurgling spring, with access to the creek bottom under
shady oaks. A graded stairway leads you out of the creek to skirt
the walls high above the canyon on the other side.

Echo Mountain appears ahead of you, signified by the tufty
tree that stands alone atop a hill. Soon you pass the ruins to your
left, where picnic tables have taken the place of roulette wheels and
manicured gardens, and turn left at the spur to take in the entire
site, perhaps perching on the grand hotel entrance stairs to survey
the tiny suburbs far below you. Heading back out to the point
where you turned off to see the sights, head straight through,
bypassing the Sam Merrill Trail, which comes down from the right
and continues to your left. Remaining on the Echo Mountain
Trail, you pass a view of the gorge (once spanned by a circular
bridge) and marvel at Sentinel Rock, a sinuous, angular formation
that was a popular sight for nineteenth-century railway patrons.
Signposts here give you more information about the old route.

You briefly join paved Sunset Ridge Road, bearing left, and
turn right 100 yards beyond at the signed Sunset Ridge Trail, with

Millard Canyon 3.5 miles ahead. The trail dips to the right by a beautiful twisted pine, and takes you very easily along a ferny hill-side, then down some wide switchbacks studded with beautiful oaks. You get more views of the city on your left about halfway along this trail. Below to your right is wild Millard Canyon, which you trekked up earlier. You find an ever-more riparian wilderness as you descend, and soon pass the start of the trail near the metal bridge and brown cabin, carrying straight through on the access road to the locked gate at the end of Chaney Trail.

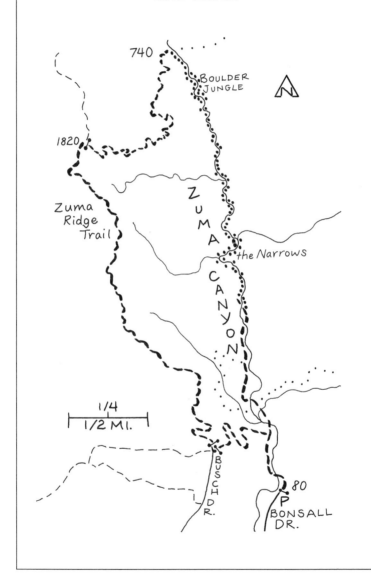

Hike 48: WILD ZUMA CANYON
AND RIDGE

740

BOULDER
JUNGLE

1820

Z
U
M
A

the Narrows

Zuma
Ridge
Trail

C
A
N
Y
O
N

1/4
1/2 MI.

B
U
S
C
H
DR.

80
P
BONSALL
DR.

↷WILD ZUMA CANYON
AND RIDGE
Level 4, Hike 48

A thoroughly challenging trailblazer's trek up the narrows of Zuma Canyon, a steep switchback climb to the ridge, and a meditative descent back to the canyon

DISTANCE: 8-mile loop; Elevation change: 1,800 feet
DURATION: 3.5–7 hours
NOTES: Dawn–dusk; highly inadvisable directly after rains; no pets permitted

DRIVING DIRECTIONS: Take PCH north to just south of Zuma Beach, turn right on Bonsall Drive, and continue at its terminus to far end of dirt parking area; no fee.

You may have already explored lower Zuma Canyon in Hike 26. Now graduate from the bunny slopes to some real freestyling. This is a hike for experts and confident novices only, since there's no trail whatsoever, and for the last two miles up the canyon plenty of low-level rock-climbing. This demanding leg is followed by a grueling climb of 1,000 feet in one mile from the creek to Zuma Ridge. To get a feel for this kind of strenuous trailblazing, make sure to navigate the half mile of similar, but slightly easier, narrows included in the tour of the Tropical Terrace Graceful Eight in Solstice Canyon (Hike 33).

Begin by swinging around the brown gate at the far end of the parking lot and walking down a dirt path much used by horses, as are all canyon-bottom trails. Continuing straight ahead on the Zuma Canyon Trail, you ignore all signs for others, and chuckle at the one declaring TRAIL ENDS, NO EXIT, .7 MILES.

The trail does end just beyond a skyscraping stand of anise to your right, and a little flat beachy place under a sycamore straight ahead of you. You may be able to find some creekside paths here and there as the canyon narrows, but your first challenge comes quite soon, as the creek makes a sharp right through sheer, close-set walls. No complicated directions here. Your simple mission: Follow the creek until you reach a trail that crosses the canyon. It's strenuous, mind-exercising work, and it's up to you to find your own best route. Take your time, always try to look ahead at least ten to twenty yards to find a clear path as you go, and stop for reconnaissance, being unafraid to backtrack whenever necessary.

You find yourself sometimes walking straight over rocks through the middle of the creek, and sometimes on barely existent trails and ledges along the creekside; sometimes bushwhacking, sometimes boulder-hopping. Stop and drink plenty of water, and eat those granola bars (or whatever it is you always bring with you but never seem to touch).

The going gets more and more rocky. Huge boulders may seem to block your path, though there is always a way around them if you are fearless and clever. As you near the trail that crosses the creek you are met with your severest challenge: a quarter mile of huge boulders that require a modicum of mountaineering ability to scale and cross. After that the creek levels out a bit, becoming merely rocky again; sycamores crowd in at the first chance of stable soil. This is your clue that the trail is nearing. You reach a wash where it crosses the creek, and take a left, beginning your steep climb up to Zuma Ridge. It's the highest point you can see way up above you, where the power lines disappear and miniature houses perch on the cliff. You are rewarded all the way up with spectacular views. The trail switches on long, earnest half-loops until you reach a dilapidated chain-link fence with a sign announcing the Zuma Ridge Trail. You turn left, toward Busch Drive.

Now you are on a long, easy descent down a wide, well-graded path toward the sea, where you can zone out and meditate on the feat you just accomplished. The bottom of Zuma Canyon opens up below you to your left, as does the suburbia of Malibu, straight ahead. Pass through a brown pipe gate after three miles on the ridge, where the road turns left, and switchbacks on long lazy hairpins down along the backside of the gracious horse-friendly ranch homes at the bottom of the hill. At Busch Drive you pass through a brown pipe gate, and head left toward the big brown slanted recycling bin, to the right of which is a small brown sign reading ZUMA CANYON ACCESS TRAIL, the last leg of your trip.

Curve right, cutting through a dilapidated fence, then make your way down quite steeply on a couple of switchbacks into the canyon, yielding to equestrians. You head for the signed Zuma Canyon Trail, turn right, and stroll, refreshed and invigorated, back to the Bonsall Drive trailhead.

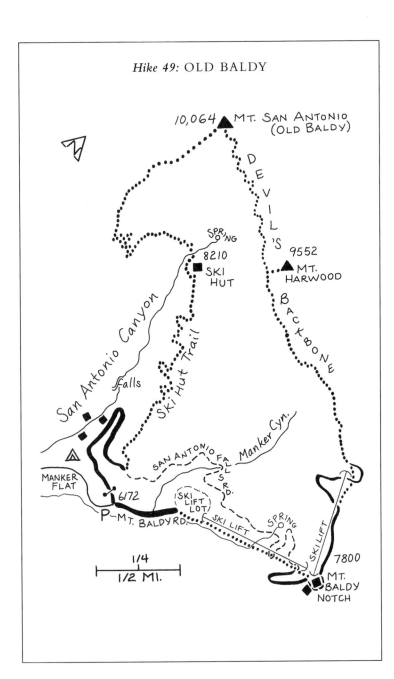

Hike 49: OLD BALDY

10,064 ▲ MT. SAN ANTONIO
(OLD BALDY)

D
E
V
I
L
'S

SPRING
8210
■ SKI
HUT

9552
▲ MT.
HARWOOD

B
A
C
K
B
O
N
E

San Antonio Canyon

Falls

Ski Hut Trail

SAN ANTONIO FALLS Manker Cyn.
RD.

Ⓐ

MANKER
FLAT

SKI LIFT
LOT

SKI LIFT

SPRING

SKI LIFT

6172

P—MT. BALDY RD.

7800

MT.
BALDY
NOTCH

1/4
1/2 MI.

⚘OLD BALDY
Level 4, Hike 49

*A long, treacherous climb to this calm vortex of a peak at over 10,000
feet, a fun twist down the Devil's Backbone, and a steep descent along the
ski lift line*

> DISTANCE: 9.4-mile loop; Elevation change: 4,000 feet
> DURATION: 3.5–7 hours
> NOTES: Dawn–dusk; highly inadvisable during winter
> months; dogs on leash permitted

DRIVING DIRECTIONS: Take the 210 Freeway east to its terminus as it blends into the 30 Freeway east, to its terminus at Foothill
Boulevard; continue east to a left (north) on Mills Avenue; shallow
right to Mt. Baldy Road at first stop sign. A steep, winding few
miles, especially just after passing the Icehouse Canyon turnoff, to
6,160 feet; park off-street where San Antonio Falls Road begins at
left (west) past Manker Flats Campground; National Forest Adventure Pass required.

Yes, that's Old Baldy, right there above you, though its apex is hidden from view slightly to the north of the granite outcroppings of
its southern slope. You begin on San Antonio Falls Road, which
leads quickly up to a vista point for this spectacular waterfall (Hike
1). You continue uphill from here on a hairpin right, following the
road to a point where it turns left. Look very closely for an
unmarked, single-track trail that leads off the main road about
twenty yards past where the road begins to veer. Last time I was

there, a plain wooden stake marked the trailhead, though this is apt to change. This is the Ski Hut Trail, leading up to the San Antonio Ski Hut, open to all and maintained beautifully by the Sierra Club (information and reservations available on the Internet at: www.off-piste.com/San%20Antonio%20Ski%20Hut/sanantonioskihut.html), about one-third of the way to the top of Mt. Baldy. You immediately begin climbing steeply along the side of the mountain, and continue as the canyon falls away below you. You may be able to see the Ski Hut far up above you between scrappy pines and jagged granite outcroppings, with its light green walls contrasting against a brilliant blue sky. The trail is narrow, rocky, and slippery, hugging the side of the mountain and then cutting into it on a series of switchbacks before skirting a series of canyon fingers. You head steeply uphill to the cabin, through fallen trees and some overgrown low-lying manzanita that enjoys water from a nearby year-round spring.

Go up and explore the hut's grounds to your right, then continue on the trail as it dips down to cross a creek. Look up to see the last few pines, redwoods, and high chaparral before the treeline. Mt. Baldy is just above you now. At this point, you begin a trek through a mountainside of granite rubble and boulders, among which the trail sometimes seems to get lost. Just a few steps, and sometimes a small amount of boulder-hopping, will always bring you back to the trail. Soon you pass a particularly fun place to cross, with huge granite boulders surrounding you, upon which you can bask in the sun like a lizard before finishing your ascent. Other hikers and maintenance volunteers have left trail markers along the way, such as piles of stones atop rocks, or edgings of small flat-faced granite slabs.

Exiting the granite wilderness, you begin a series of sharp, tight switchbacks to the south crest of Mt. Baldy, which lies behind the huge granite outcroppings you see above you. Oh boy, is the air clean up here. Take a few deep breaths.

A bit more granite scaling introduces you to the final part of this climb, the steepest 4,000 feet you will ever ascend. Make sure to keep your energy up on this hike with trail mix, etc., and drink plenty of water, especially since the altitude here may wreak havoc on your system.

The last few hundred feet are extremely hard going. As you near the top, a series of granite outcroppings invites you to frequent rests. You reach a saddle and see that Mt. Baldy is still ahead of you. Climbing the last section of barren trail to the top, you are greeted by a single stubby pine. At the bare, lonely apex, large clumps of rocks have been built as windbreaks. The old metal sign reads, SAN ANTO-NIO/MT. BALDY, ELEV. 10,064. Stunning views surround you. You may be visited by silently swooping bluebirds as you eat a celebratory granola bar. Listen: This is probably the quietest place in all of Los Angeles County. It is also one of the windiest, and you have to take into account a twenty- or thirty-degree temperature drop due to the extremely high altitude when packing extra layers to don and doff.

Once warmed, rested, and reenergized, begin down the signed Devil's Backbone to Ski Lift Trail, heading east on the ridge along a bare, twisted, rocky spine. Views and natural delights continue all the way down on this high, windy, lonesome trail. You soon find yourself again among mountain manzanita and treeline firs. After thirty to fifty minutes of descent, you round a bend to see the ski lift outpost buildings below you on a flat area. Look down to your right to see Mt. Baldy Road far below you, specks of cars scurrying along it like insects. Both the terrain and the plant life get more varied again as you descend. You pass a rest area, and the upper terminus of the ski lift appears before you, accompanied by signs reading SKI AREA BOUNDARY, NO DOWNHILL LOADING. Continue on the trail as it widens, going past the ski lift to the left. As you near the brown building with the turquoise tanks in the flat below, you come to a place where the main road goes downhill and to the right, and a shortcut goes straight ahead—this shortcut (and others along this wide, winding trail that roughly follows the ski lift down to the road) is very steep, so hook a sharp right here if you don't want to pound the soles of your feet into hamburger. At the end of the road you come to a big plateau housing the Mt. Baldy Ski School and a rental shop. Proceed through, bearing right, and turn right between the school and the rental shop to begin your final descent to Manker Flats.

Shortly you see the second leg of the ski lift running down to the bottom of the mountain. The fire road winds weirdly down the hill on elongated half-loops, basically following the path of the ski lift to San Antonio Falls Road and your starting point. I suggest one more adventure here: As you can see, supersteep little foot trails cut off all the lazy loops of the access road, tumbling down the rocky hillside just beneath the ski lift. Go ahead and take this if you are feeling wild and surefooted and up for one more thrill. Balance and footing are of the utmost importance as you make your way, sometimes jogging, perhaps enduring a light fall here and there, all the way down to the ski lift entrance. At the bottom, head left to find a narrow footpath that continues down to Manker Flats past the boring maze of the many-tiered parking lot, a couple hundred yards beyond which your car is parked at the corner of San Antonio Falls Road. Go ahead, take the plunge: It makes the end of the trip as exciting as the beginning, creating a vivid, joyous symmetry.

❧ RUSTIC CANYON TREK
Level 4, Hike 50

A steady, sky-filled climb up the Backbone Trail to Temescal Ridge, a steep descent through a bay-filled tributary, and a few miles of acrobatic trailblazing through wild and wooly lower Rustic Canyon back to Will Rogers State Historic Park

DISTANCE: 15-mile loop; Elevation change: 1,500 feet
DURATION: 5–8.5 hours
NOTES: 8 A.M.–5 P.M.; highly inadvisable directly after rains; no pets permitted

DRIVING DIRECTIONS: Take Sunset Boulevard west to the Pacific Palisades area, turn right on traffic-lighted Will Rogers Drive at the sign for Will Rogers State Historic Park, just past Amalfi Drive. In just under a mile, you reach the entrance. Park in the first, lower lot; $3 fee.

From the far side of the parking lot, take the Parking Lot Spur Trail to the Inspiration Point Loop Trail, and continue to the glorious views of Inspiration Point, where your adventure officially begins. The first half involves a perfectly agreeable climb up the pleasant Backbone Trail to the Temescal Ridge area, and then it's down on a slippery, narrow trail to Rustic Canyon, where you will find out just how rustic it is by trailblazing, not difficult in terms of navigation but requiring semi-acrobatic feats to circumvent obstacles, the first few miles down to the lower canyon trails.

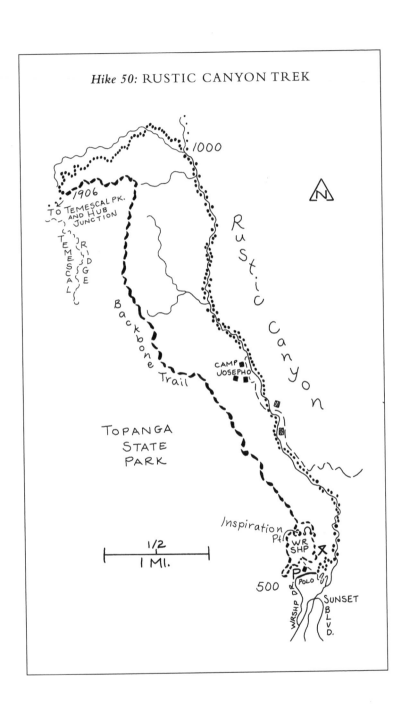

Hike 50: RUSTIC CANYON TREK

1000

1906

TO TEMESCAL PK.
AND HUB
JUNCTION

TEMESCAL RIDGE

Rustic Canyon

Backbone Trail

CAMP JOSEPHO

TOPANGA
STATE
PARK

Inspiration
Pt.

WR
SHP

X

1/2

1 MI.

500

P

POLO

WRSHP DR.

SUNSET
BLVD.

Turning onto the Backbone Trail at Inspiration Point, you proceed along a lazy ridge to climb just over 1,200 feet in five miles—a nice, unstrenuous ascent along a shaded, well-marked path. Temescal Ridge appears in the distance, a string of telephone poles running along its spine. You play hide and seek with Encino in the valley far to your north through the clefts in the mountain range, heading across Temescal Canyon and curving up to the left. If you continue on the road, you reach the Temescal Ridge Trail and Hub Junction, which you traversed in Hike 37. Before the ridge, look closely to your right for a brown sign reading, simply, TRAIL, nearly hidden by foliage. Turn right onto the unidentified Baytree Trail here, which winds downhill steeply at first, then threads through manzanita and oak archways. Watch your head for snags and branches. This is very much like the wicked queen's forest in the Disney version of *Snow White and the Seven Dwarfs*, full of low, grabbing boughs. Because it is not a well-traveled trail it can be quite overgrown in places. It also gets mushy on its left border, which gives way to a steep, slippery hillside, so watch your footing. You may frighten a big stag or a doe and her fawns out of the thick trees and brush.

After thirty to forty-five minutes on this somewhat treacherous trail, you come to a deep, shady, almost dark-as-night ravine full of young and stunted eucalyptus and bay trees. The eucalyptus stays so moist that it remains heartily fragrant throughout the year. Soon after, you crouch through a series of overgrown scrub oak and bay trees to the Rustic Canyon creekbed, and find that you basically have to sit down and slide a short way down a sheer bank to reach it. Once in, turn right, using the creek itself as your only navigational tool. While this trek is most enjoyable and easily accomplished in the summer when the creek is dry, it can be navigated when there is some water in the creek. Never attempt it dur-

ing winter rains or the early spring, when the stream swells to a
depth of up to six feet through impassable banks.

. Watch out for poison oak the entire way down. You may feel
you're the only person who has ever been down here. It's a wild
and amazing landscape: cool, shady, and sometimes eerily silent,
with many strange, hidden cubbyholes and cavelets to explore. You
are alone with the lizards, crickets, frogs, deer, snakes, and birds
down here. The creekbed is wide, and sometimes seems impassable,
but there is always a way onward. You will find yourself practicing
either the hurdles or the limbo getting over and under trees that
have fallen across the creek, or simply grown low and swoopy from
one side to the other. Even more tricky than the trees, though, are
the number of immense spiderwebs, some of them still actively
guarded by their large brown or black builders, but mostly abandoned, under which you must crouch at several points during your
journey. You will most likely be nearly mummified in sticky web
detritus by the time you begin to spot the first signs of civilization.

These appear in the form of a couple of outhouses, some picnic tables, and a sign that reads NO TRESPASSING as you near the still-
active Camp Josepho Boy Scout facility. A bit after the sign, a road
dips up out of the creek. Follow it as it dwindles to a path past a
pool, an amphitheater, a water tank, and many of the buildings of
this large, popular campground. Instead of following one of the
roads leading all the way through the camp, cut down to the creek
again and find one of the many foot trails that lace the creek as it
cuts through the camp. Remain closest to the creek when you
come to forks for the best exploring.

Keep to your left as the Backbone Trail leads off to the right.
You pass an old white barn surrounded by a chain-link and barbed-
wire fence and continue creekside as the stream, even in dry months,
now runs with water. You run across some of the few blackberry

brambles in Southern California here, though they never really do get completely ripe. Farther down, the stream runs even stronger. This is as close to jungle as California comes. Just past a manger and a set of unused stables, the trail veers left, then right around a dammed waterfall into lower Rustic Canyon. Here your first well-marked path in quite a while begins on a little wooden stairwell that takes you down to the creek, then winds back and forth, and back again across the stream, sometimes requiring shallow wading or rock-hopping. Reachable through the eastern side of Will Rogers State Historic Park, this lower part of Rustic Canyon is a great place to explore, play, and picnic with children.

The creek by now has become an active brook. After some fairly treacherous stream-hopping, suburbia appears above you to your left while the trail rises up, across the stream to the right, to a wooden post-lined pathway that goes far up above the creek and winds along the side of the canyon back to Will Rogers State Historic Park.

Pass a stable, hairpin up to the right, then left, cross a small bridge near an interesting rock formation, and hairpin up again. The fence has fallen down here and there along the steep walls below the trail, so watch your footing and balance. Crossing over a few canyon fingerlets, you peek into some residential paradises, cross another bridge and a miniature ravine, and soon spot the huge green polo grounds of the park through eucalypti. Following the road you come to on your right, past the picnic grounds and the house toward the parking lot, you see that all the trash cans and tables of Will Rogers State Historic Park are stencil-painted with the acronym "WRSHP," which may start to look like a personalized license-plate version of "worship" on some religious person's car; in this environment, it simply reminds you what you actually do when you commune with nature as deeply as you have just done.

Appendix:
A Lost and Magical Weekend
in Montaña de Oro State Park

To reach Montaña de Oro State Park, take the 101 Freeway north from L.A. approximately 200 miles to the Los Osos Valley Road exit. Head west ten miles to where the road curves left at the Los Osos Valley Nursery (you will see the sand dunes ahead of you), and continue on a more winding road for four-plus miles through California's oldest stand of eucalyptus trees to the heart of the park at Spooner's Cove, a small bay with a central hillock and a wide bluff beyond it; a ranger's station and campground lie to its left. Take the road just past the cove, and park in the off-street dirt parking turnoff to your right; no fee. No-hook-up, cold-water campground usage costs $8 per day should you wish to spend the night.

I include this full day or weekend trip to the central coast of California mainly because Montaña de Oro ("Golden Mountain") has always been one of my favorite places. It also happens to be a perfect getaway from Los Angeles, with its long, meditative drive up the Ventura Freeway to a coastal landscape like no other. Wild, yet calming, with high bluffs, deep coves, and a seven-mile strand of soft, tilted sedimentary rock leading to a string of large sand dunes, the park is one of California's largest, covering over 8,000 acres.

The seemingly endless eucalyptus groves that fill the park between coast and mountains were planted in the mid-nineteenth century by an entrepreneur named Hazard who planned to cash in on the growing timber needs of the new state with his fast-growing crop. Unfortunately, eucalyptus, native to Australia, twists as it grows in the northern hemisphere, proving unsatisfactory for milling. The trees' pungent fragrance permeates the park, mixing with the gentle mists that often cover it, along with the sharp, lively smell of the sea.

Otters, seals, pelicans, and other entertaining seaside wildlife are commonplace here, and humpback whales or dolphins can often be seen out to sea from the many spectacular lookouts on the bluffs. Deer, rabbits, foxes, hawks, and other inland animals run about everywhere, making it one of the best wildlife-spotting areas on the West Coast. Looking more closely at the ocean, a long string of tide-pools begins at the central outcropping in Spooner's Cove, and continues through the smaller coves all the way south beneath the bluff, providing hours, even days, of entertainment for explorers of all ages. Don't remove starfish (or any other plant or animal life, for that matter), and don't stick your finger in the middle of a sea anemone if it's bigger than your head, as you may not be able to extract it.

Throughout the park, middens, mounds, and other traces of the gentle Chumash Indian culture that flourished in this area until the eighteenth century can still be found, and the long, lonely dunes can be walked along for hours, through an expansive salt marsh also rife with wildlife, to monolithic Morro Rock, the central coast's most recognizable landmark, home to an ongoing California Condor repopulation project.

Be sure to dress in layers as the climate is wildly changeable here, and make a night of it in the campground or one of the many quirky little local motels if you are as enchanted as I have always been with this wonderland.

Hike 51: MONTAÑA DE ORO
PEAKS AND BLUFFS

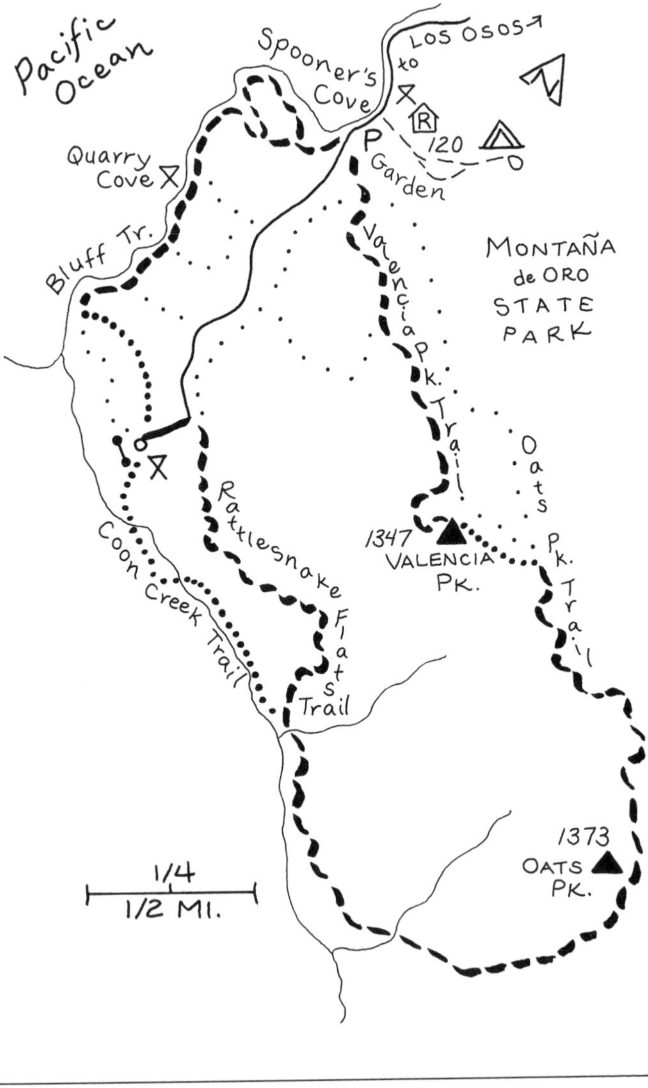

Pacific Ocean

Spooner's Cove

LOS OSOS→

to

Quarry Cove

P

Garden

120

R

Bluff Tr.

MONTAÑA
de ORO
STATE
PARK

Valencia Pk. Trail

Oats Pk. Trail

Rattlesnake Flats Trail

1347
VALENCIA PK.

Coon Creek Trail

1373
OATS PK.

1/4
1/2 MI.

⚘MONTAÑA DE ORO
PEAKS AND BLUFFS
Level 3, Hike 51

A quick climb to a peak with magnificent views, a scrabble along a ridge, then down through coastal scrub to walk a carved-bluff wilderness

DISTANCE: 7-mile loop; Elevation change: 1,300 feet
DURATION: 2–4 hours
NOTES: Dawn–dusk; no pets permitted on trails

Just next to your signed starting point across the street from the parking area past the ranger station on the Valencia Peak Trail is the Betty Holloway Memorial Garden, an excellent interpretive spread of the coastal chaparral environment. This is a good place to become thoroughly familiar with the habitat through which you are about to trek, which also prevails in coastal areas throughout the L.A. region.

Starting up on the Valencia Peak Trail, on clear days you can see for miles and miles out into the swelling blue and purple ocean. On the area's frequent foggy mornings you won't even be able to see the peak that you are approaching, but there is an idiosyncratic magic to scaling a peak in the midst of a cloud. Quiet surrounds you, and spiderwebs glisten like diamond necklaces strung between the brittle branches of yarrow and sage. At the second fork, about thirty to fifty minutes into your hike, you turn right, keeping on the main trail. Ten or fifteen minutes later you reach the zenith of Valencia Peak at 1,347 feet. At the top, as you face the ocean, or, if you're enveloped in the soft quiet of a cloud, as you face the ampersand in the U.S. Coast & Geodetic Survey

Triangulation Station, there is a trail just to your left and slightly behind you. This leads you down the spine of the ridge to the next apex at Oats Peak, 1,373 feet. Find your favorite hiding place in the many rocky crags here; space is available even when the peak is somewhat crowded on sunny summer days.

Bearing left at the next small fork, continue down, wobbling on a slippery trail of broken rock. You scale a hillock to elegant manzanita trees blown landward by the coastal winds, and into a much brushier area, then wind down the southerly hillside. Next you pass a gorge, and head toward the sea. As you can see from this vantage point there are numerous trails leading all over the place below you to your left and ahead of you on the bluff.

Complete families of deer bound and leap across your path. Coveys of quail take flight, sounding like armies of helicopters, as you frighten them out of their bushy hiding places.

Continue down toward the ocean, where the trail gets sandy, leading to the main paved road through the park. Turn left, toward a locked perimeter gate and a restroom area. Across from the parking turnout there is a trail leading out to the bluffs, designated by a sign prohibiting dogs and horses. You head toward the ocean and reach the head of the bluff, where you may spot seals garlanded with kelp, or otters floating on their backs fumbling with mussels. An array of hawks and the occasional eagle flies past, or settles on a complicated, wind-sculpted sandstone and shale outcropping.

Turn right on the trail at the edge of the bluff, which leads you past many opportunities for hearty sidetrips back to your car. Spend as much time as possible breathing the sea air, feeling the strong pulse of the ocean here as it continues to carve coves into the cliffs of the bluff, and taking all the little sidetrails that lead out to the edges of the cliffs, or down to hidden coves, beaches, and rock formations. This is one of the greatest places on the California coast for exploration. There are so many wonderful things to find here that I'm not going to give it all away. A regular smattering of local birdwatchers, fishermen, mountain bikers, joggers, and powerwalkers use this trail as their main hobbyist artery. You may choose to commune more casually with the birds and bunnies and butterflies, or have a picnic in one of the less easily reached secret coves.

At the end of the bluff the trail curves up toward the road to the parking area. Below you to your left is Spooner's Cove, an excellent place to rest before your next hike, with a carefully scalable rocky centerpiece perfect for big kids and amateur climbers.

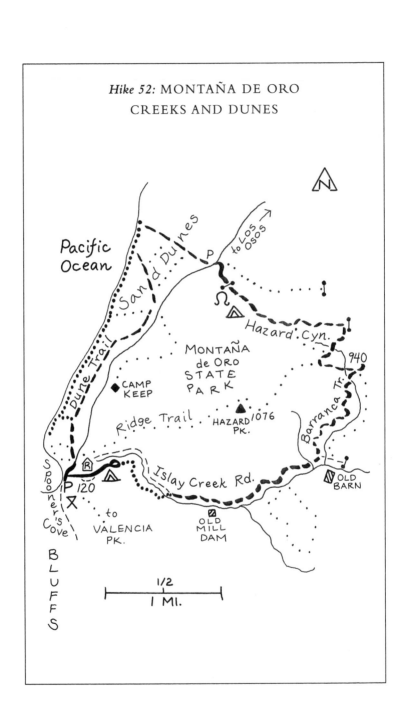

Hike 52: MONTAÑA DE ORO
CREEKS AND DUNES

Pacific
Ocean

Sand Dunes

to Los Osos

P

Hazard Cyn.

MONTAÑA
de ORO
STATE
PARK

Dune Trail

CAMP
KEEP

Ridge Trail

HAZARD 1076
PK.

940

Barranca Tr.

OLD
BARN

Spooner's Cove

P 120

Islay Creek Rd.

to
VALENCIA
PK.

OLD
MILL
DAM

B
L
U
F
F
S

1/2
1 MI.

❧ MONTAÑA DE ORO
CREEKS AND DUNES
Level 4, Hike 52

An overgrown creek, a steep climb, a canyon exploration, a dune crossing, and rock hopping down the rugged strand, then back through the dunes to Spooner's Cove

DISTANCE: 10-mile complicated loop; Elevation change: 1,000 feet

DURATION: 3.5–6 hours

NOTES: Dawn–dusk; no pets permitted on trails

Take a rest, spend the night, or do some automotive sightseeing after your first hike, or join both hikes for a challenging all-day trek.

Begin by taking the road that leads east past the ranger's station through the campground, all the way down to the end at site 40. Here you see the Reservoir Flats trailhead, and swing around the poles through the entryway. You traverse a lush hillside above a riparian wilderness. Below is Islay Creek, overgrown and fragile; really too fragile for human exploration, so stay on the trail. Watch out for copious stinging nettle and poison oak.

Around half an hour later you hit a junction with a slightly larger trail. You continue in the same direction down into the creek canyon, curving around and down, then hitting another junction. The left trail takes you into the creekbed, and the right to a hideaway farther upstream. Take the trail to the left, using whatever rocks or logs are available to cross the small stream. The trail continues on the other side of the creek, climbing steeply up out of the bed to the Islay Creek Trail, a much wider dirt path used also by equestrians and bicyclists. Turning left will take you straight back to Spooner's Cove. You turn right and head up the canyon.

Soon after you see a small waterfall down below you. It's not accessible, alas, but it provides a beautiful show and soothing soundtrack as you pass.

Fifteen to twenty-five minutes later, look closely for the Barranca Trail, a small footpath leading up to your left. Here you turn to wind uphill, gently at first, then steeply to an apex at the eastern edge of the park. On this trail, even on a very overcast day, you leave the clouds behind and warm under the sun and blue sky, with excellent views of the coastal range. At the top of this trail you see a tool stand, filled with shovels and rakes. From the accompanying placard: "Tools for volunteer trail maintenance on the Barranca Trail. If you regularly use this trail, please consider taking a little time to help keep it clean and erosion-free. Tools are provided by the Central Coast Concerned Mountain Bikers with help from the Atascadero Horsemen and support from the Montaña de Oro State Park staff."

At the top you are rewarded with a picnic table shaded by oak and twisted manzanita trees. You continue downhill after visiting the peak, through a landscape where chaparral gives way to a variety of trees. Beyond you is the fence outlining the park boundary.

Soon you come to a junction. You turn left on the East Boundary Trail, even though there is no arrow indicating flow of traffic in this direction. You get your first glimpse of the ocean for a while on this segment.

At the next junction take the right fork, continuing downward on the East Boundary Trail. Just a few feet after that you come to a fork for the Manzanita Trail, where you turn right again. A couple of minutes later you reach yet another fork, and another right turn, continuing once again on the East Boundary Trail. Soon you find yourself descending into a lush stream and marsh area right along the barbed-wire boundary fence. The trail turns left at a clearing, heading toward the sea.

You descend down the canyon on a wide dirt trail with stands of eucalyptus to your left, explorable via one-way spur trails. Around the second grove, you see the outskirts of the large Montaña de Oro horse camp. You continue just above the camp to the right. On your left near the end of the camp you swing around a fence and continue, the trail winding up slightly to the main road through the park.

Cross the road and head slightly to your left, about fifty yards, to a small parking turnoff, where you turn right, straight down on the sandy trail all the way through the dunes to the beach. Wend your way down any way you can, heeding the signs that read FRAGILE AREA, STAY ON TRAIL—dune vegetation is easily destructible, hanging on for dear life in the shifting sands. A single footprint in this ecosystem can change it radically. The sand here makes you feel like you're walking on a planet with a much higher gravity.

Once down on the beach, you turn left to walk along the wide strand. If you look to your right you can see Morro Rock and its three attendant smokestacks seven miles north up the coast. The strand and dunes are walkable all the way to a narrow bay passage lane that separates them from the rock. Heading left, you'll be going back toward Spooner's Cove, right along the beach. At the end of the beach you hit a rocky point, and continue on, doing some slight rock-hopping along tilted, fault-formed slate slabs, jutting up like great lost tablets from the annals of a dead civilization. You make it almost all the way to Spooner's Cove. Go as far as possible, as this is one of the wildest, most engaging coastal environments you're likely to have the pleasure of exploring.

As you near the cove, you may see a few small forts or wigwams built out of the extra-large pieces of eucalyptus driftwood that wash up here. If so, sit in one and leave a sign of your visit, or build your own if you like.

You eventually hit an impassable (except by swimming) stretch between this strand of rocky outcroppings and Spooner's Cove. Backtrack a bit and find a way to scramble up the dunes to the small trails that will wind you back to Spooner's Cove landward. The unavoidable impassability looms around the area where the rocks begin to resemble large flat discs or ancient wheels. If you look closely you'll see a steep trail between two high cliffs of dune in a rocky cove between two small peninsulas, usually muddy because the tide can sometimes reach right up to it.

Wind your way up, channeling through deer, horse, and hiking trails. The small poles that look like hitching posts are actually barriers for sliding sands and their attached sliding vegetation. The main dunes trail can be found over the first row of dunes, quite near the road. It leads you toward the cove, with a view before you and slightly to your left of Valencia Peak. Just over the next ridge of dunes, you follow the telephone wires to Spooner's Cove. The trail deposits you on the main road just before it dips down to the cove, right above which your car is parked, and the more vegetated dunes leading to your right from here, extending high above the cove, are explorable on their own playful web of footpaths.

Part 3

⚜

Special
Recommendations

Hikes and sections of hikes that are highly recommended for . . .

1. Families, Small Children, and Elders

All hikes in Level 1, plus . . .

2. Picnicking

3. A Workout

All hikes are good workouts; these are highly recommended . . .

4. A Thrill

5. Romantic Outings

6. Meditation

*As with workouts, all hikes are good for meditation. These are
the best . . .*

7. Breathtaking Views

8. Summer Coolness

9. Spring Wildflowers

10. Autumn Leaves

11. **Wildlife Sightings**

12. Spectacular Sunsets

Not all spectacular sunsets happen at the beach . . .